Observing and Developing Schematic Behaviour in Young Children

of related interest

Positive Behaviour Management in Early Years Settings
An Essential Guide
Liz Williams
ISBN 978 1 78592 026 4
eISBN 978 1 78450 273 7

Listening to Young Children, Expanded Third Edition
The Mosaic Approach
Alison Clark
Foreword by Peter Moss
ISBN 978 1 90939 122 2
eISBN 978 1 90939 126 0

Learning through Movement and Active Play in the Early Years
A Practical Resource for Professionals and Teachers
Tania Swift
ISBN 978 1 78592 085 1
eISBN 978 1 78450 346 8

Promoting Young Children's Emotional Health and Wellbeing
A Practical Guide for Professionals and Parents
Sonia Mainstone-Cotton
ISBN 978 1 78592 054 7
eISBN 978 1 78450 311 6

Observing and Developing Schematic Behaviour in Young Children

A Professional's Guide for Supporting Children's Learning, Play and Development

Tamsin Grimmer

Jessica Kingsley *Publishers*
London and Philadelphia

First published in 2017
by Jessica Kingsley Publishers
73 Collier Street
London N1 9BE, UK
and
400 Market Street, Suite 400
Philadelphia, PA 19106, USA

www.jkp.com

Library of Congress Cataloging in Publication Data
A CIP catalog record for this book is available from the Library of Congress

British Library Cataloguing in Publication Data
A CIP catalogue record for this book is available from the British Library

ISBN 978 1 78592 179 7
eISBN 978 1 78450 450 2

Printed and bound by CPI Group (UK) Ltd, Croydon, CR0 4YY

MIX
Paper from
responsible sources
FSC
www.fsc.org   FSC® C013604

This book is dedicated to my amazing children who have inspired me with their schematic behaviour: Pippa, Hannah and Becky.

Contents

Acknowledgements

This book only exists because of the generosity of all the parents who have given their kind permission for me to include stories and photographs about their wonderful children. I would like to particularly thank my husband for supporting me whilst I was writing and my mum for her dedication to proofreading and for her constant encouragement. I would also like to thank the team at Jessica Kingsley Publishers for their support.

About the Author

Tamsin Grimmer is an experienced and excellent independent consultant and trainer and one of the directors of Linden Learning. Tamsin is passionate about young children's learning and development and is fascinated by how very young children think. She believes that all children deserve practitioners who are inspiring, dynamic, reflective and passionate about teaching them and has a keen interest in the different ways that children learn. Tamsin is particularly interested in play, schemas, active learning, promoting positive behaviour and supporting early language development. In her spare time, Tamsin is in her final year of studying for a Masters Degree in Early Childhood Education at the University of Chester.

Introduction

Tuning into children's interests and fascinations is part of daily practice for those working with or caring for young children. We watch the children as they play, sometimes from a distance as an observer and sometimes while we participate in the play with them. Children are often engaged in play that is repetitive in nature, for example lining up their toys, or they show a particular fascination with something, for example a keen interest in wheels. It is these repeated patterns of behaviour that are often referred to as schemas.

The term 'schemas' is not widely understood, and can be mysterious to many working within the early years sector and to the majority of parents and carers. There is almost an air of smoke and mirrors about this theme. In fact, most childcare qualifications and parenting courses do not mention schemas, yet these repeated behaviours of children continually intrigue and perplex the adults who care for them and an understanding of schemas helps to interpret this behaviour. I hope that this book will clarify the term and make schemas more accessible to those working with or looking after young children.

I have observed that there can be a very academic slant in books on schemas and schematic behaviour, with theorists using language which I view to be inaccessible to many and rather technical (e.g. forms of thought, horizontal, dynamic schemas). For the purposes of this book, I take a more practical approach. I consider the action or movement that is repeated (connection, transporting, rotation, etc.) and I have chosen the terms that are already widely used to avoid any confusion. This should provide clarity and generally make schemas and schematic behaviour better understood. Many of the case studies I discuss in this book are children who I have studied over time. I have also included a Glossary which explains key words and phrases used in this book. These words are italicised in the text the first time they appear in the text.

What is a schema? The theory

Schematic behaviour has been researched, discussed and studied over the years by many theorists. Piaget[1] is possibly one of the earliest and most widely recognised theorists who referred to patterns of behaviour or schemas in relation to thought and action. He believed that when young children repeat actions, they are able to transfer their ideas into similar situations or generalise them into early concepts about the world around them. Theorists sometimes call this idea 'forms of thought', which are ways of organising our thinking to help us to make sense of the world.

Other theorists suggest schemas are 'like pieces of ideas or concepts'.[2] This can be compared with children doing a jigsaw. They do not yet have all of the pieces so they try to make sense of the jigsaw according to the pieces they do have. Through repeating different actions, children are able to investigate whether what they think happens will happen again. If they were right, the jigsaw piece fits; if they were wrong, they may need to rethink and get another jigsaw piece.

Chris Athey defined schema as 'a pattern of repeatable behaviour'.[3] Piaget and Athey believed that schematic behaviour leads children to develop ideas and concepts which form the basis of their understanding. Through exploration, children are able to generalise about objects, categorise and classify their properties and make assumptions about why things happen and how things work. Children are like scientists who are doing experiments methodically and investigating carefully in order to test their theories.[4]

For example, when a child first learns to recognise a duck, they have made connections in their brain about the 'duck-ness' of ducks. The repeated experience of seeing ducks confirms this. However, when introduced to a chicken for the first time, they may call it a 'duck', demonstrating their schema of thought and the similarities that they have noticed. The new information about chickens requires them to unlearn or rather fine-tune their earlier thinking and recognise the subtle differences between chickens and ducks.

Athey[3] talks about that 'eureka' moment when a child makes a leap forward in their knowledge, and she and Piaget use the terms *assimilation* to describe when new information is incorporated into existing schemas and *accommodation* to describe when schemas are adapted or altered to accommodate the new information. This information may consolidate their existing schema and confirm its validity, or it could question it, necessitating children to rethink or unlearn. Brierley explains that children need to be capable of unlearning so that their brains are not 'fixed in a wrong response'.[5] This rethinking and reframing as a result of assimilation is highlighted in the duck/chicken example above. The child needs to go through the process of accommodation and change their schematic thinking about ducks to incorporate the new information about chickens.

When children are engaging in schematic play, they are usually experimenting with what they can do unaided or independently. When we support and extend schemas, we aim to do so in Vygotsky's *Zone of Proximal Development*, which is what children can do with additional support.[6] This has also been called *scaffolding*, when adults support children to move towards a greater or deeper understanding of an idea or concept. It is important to tune into the language that children are using and the way they mark-make or create representations of their thinking. Cathy Nutbrown unpicked this idea in her book *Threads of Thinking* when she interpreted observations of children collated over a ten-year period.[7] Tuning into children's language can provide an important insight into their schemas.

We can also talk to children about their learning and ask open-ended questions about what they are doing. This is engaging in *sustained shared thinking* with children and will support and extend children's schematic play. Sustained shared thinking is a fairly new term that arose out of the Effective Provision in Pre-school Education (EPPE) research project[8] and refers to when children work with an adult or more able peer to solve a problem or clarify and extend their thinking. We build on what children can do and extend their thinking by questioning, offering ideas or additional resources or through playing alongside and modelling a different approach.

It is important when questioning children that we do so in a developmentally appropriate way. Open-ended questions are the best sort to further engage children with the thinking process, however, according to Marion Blank[9] it is better to use more concrete questions with younger children and move towards more abstract questions as children develop. For example, questions for babies and toddlers may include 'What is that?', 'What can you see?' or more closed questions such as 'What is...doing?' or 'Is it a...?' Questions for three- to four-year-olds might involve some analysis and progress to 'What is happening in this picture?' or 'Find something that is ...and...'

Questions for a child aged four to five could include predictions, 'What will happen next?', or encourage thinking about the perspective of others, 'How do you think he feels?' These questions are more challenging and require higher-order thinking skills as they are more abstract. Questions for children over five years old can incorporate problem solving, predictions, solutions and explanations. This requires children to use their own knowledge and thinking in order to answer the question. For example, 'What will happen if...?', 'What should we do now?' and, 'How did that happen?'

Let's think about what this looks like for a child. Consider Liam, a fairly typical four-year-old boy who has an interest in wheels and things that rotate (see Chapter 11 on rotation). We can scaffold his learning by offering him a simple problem to solve – how do we attach the wheels to this car? Or extend his thinking by providing a selection of wheels to explore and investigate, for example, why do big wheels turn more slowly than small wheels? When Liam saw his grandad's car stuck in the mud, he was very interested in watching the wheels spin round and round. We might ask Liam questions such as, 'Why do you think the wheel was spinning so fast but the car wasn't moving?' and 'How can we help the car to move again?', which is engaging in sustained shared thinking with him. This is problem solving and cooperative thinking, when children and adults can together think deeply about a problem or puzzling scenario.

Schemas within early years frameworks

In England, schemas very nearly became part of the statutory framework within the early years sector. The glossary in the Early Years Foundation Stage (EYFS) consultation document[10] contained a comprehensive definition of schemas:

> Schemas are patterns of repeated behaviour in children. Children often have a very strong drive to repeat actions such as moving things from one place to another, covering things up and putting things into containers, or moving in circles or throwing things. These patterns can often be observed running through their play and vary between one child and another. If practitioners build on these interests powerful learning can take place.

This definition describes schemas in terms of children's actions and suggests the strength in learning when these interests are extended. If this had been included in the final statutory framework, it could have been helpful for practitioners who perhaps see schemas as an inaccessible academic tool and not something they feel able to engage with.[11] Unfortunately, when the EYFS was published in 2008, it did not include this reference to schemas. When the EYFS was revised in 2012, 2014,[12] and again in 2017,[13] these were further opportunities to include schemas and schematic behaviour in a statutory framework; however, schemas were largely absent to the untrained eye. A more experienced practitioner may interpret the idea of considering individual needs, interests and stage of development of each child as also incorporating schemas and schematic behaviour.

The English non-statutory guidance, Development Matters,[14] refers to schemas in the positive relationships section for children aged 16–26 months. Practitioners are taught, within the EYFS, to consider the content of what they provide for young children, in terms of an enabling environment and positive relationships. It is also important to observe children's thought processes in an attempt to understand their thinking.

To the best of my knowledge, schemas are not officially incorporated into any early childhood programmes or curriculums in the UK or overseas. In the Republic of Ireland they briefly feature in the research paper, 'Supporting early learning and development through formative assessment', with an entry in the glossary defining schemas as 'patterns of early repeatable behaviours which children engage in and which lead them through a process of co-ordination, to make generalisations'.[15]

Using this book

This book aims to enable childcare professionals, teachers, parents and carers to understand and identify children's repeated patterns of behaviour and to learn different ways that they can further support their children. Chapter 1 looks briefly at how we learn, including a basic introduction to the brain and how repeated experiences, such as schematic behaviour, reinforce synapses. Chapter 2 goes on to share the general principles of observation and some practical hints and tips when identifying schemas.

Chapters 3–14 unpick the most commonly observed schemas in turn, one per chapter. I have chosen these particular schemas because they appear to me to be the most widely known and recognised patterns of behaviour. Each of these chapters includes photos, case studies and cameos which demonstrate children engaged in each particular schema or repetitive behaviour. These case studies are then interpreted and information is shared about how to extend children's learning and development in ways that relate to the identified schema. I have divided these chapters into sections under the headings, 'What? Observing the (name) schema', 'So what? Interpreting the (name) schema' and 'What next? Extending the (name) schema'. Providing children with opportunities to consolidate their schemas will help them to further understand a concept.[1] It is my hope that reading this book will enable practitioners to support children to do this.

I have also included some information about how each schema might link to other schemas. Sometimes these links are clear and many children display behaviours that are difficult to assign to one particular schema because they seem to fit into several. Schemas can develop in clusters when children appear to be following multiple schemas at the same time. Children with similar schemas often play together using their schematic play as a shared interest. It is important to remember that not all children will engage in schematic play; some children will never follow obvious schemas.

For the purposes of this book I have tried to discuss individual schemas and isolate schematic behaviour in order to highlight each schema individually. However, in reality, we cannot separate schematic play into neat boxes, as previously mentioned. For example, if a child builds an enclosure for animals, is this evidence of an enclosing schema or evidence of a connecting schema? It could easily be either of them or even both. Sometimes there are blurred lines between the different schemas and therefore each chapter is designed to be read in conjunction with the other chapters rather than in isolation. It doesn't really matter what the name of the schema is, the key is to observe the play, interpret it and then plan future learning opportunities based around the repetitive play observed. This is the widely recognised observation cycle that is mentioned in Chapter 2.

Sometimes children's repeated patterns of behaviour are perplexing or can be misunderstood by both practitioners and parents to be misbehaviour or naughtiness. Chapter 15 encourages practitioners and parents to reinterpret this behaviour in a positive light based on their knowledge of schemas. By recognising certain behaviour as schematic, we can divert children's attention away from the unwanted behaviour to other activities which would also be linked to their schema. Distraction alone is not always enough for some children. However linking the alternative suggestion to a child's fascination may well do the trick.

I hope that this book unpicks schemas and makes them more accessible to those caring for or looking after young children, so that they might be viewed as effective learners exploring and investigating the world around them.

References

1. Piaget, J. and Cook, M. T. (1952) *The Origins of Intelligence in Children*. New York: International University Press.
2. Meade, A. and Cubey, P. (2008) *Thinking Children: Learning about Schemas*. Maidenhead: Open University.
3. Athey, C. (2007) *Extending Thought in Young Children: A Parent–Teacher Partnership* (2nd ed.). London: Sage.
4. Gopnik, A. (2010) 'How babies think.' *Scientific American* 303, 1, 76–81.
5. Brierley, B. (1987) *Give Me a Child until He is Seven*. Barcombe: Falmer.
6. Vygotsky, L. (1978) *Mind in society: The development of higher psychological processes*. Cambridge, MA: Harvard University Press.
7. Nutbrown, C. (2011) *Threads of Thinking* (4th ed.). London: Sage.
8. Silva, K. (2010) 'Quality in Early Childhood Settings.' In K. Silva, E. Melhuish, P. Sammons, I. Siraj-Blatchford, and B. Taggart (eds) *Early Childhood Matters: Evidence from the Effective Pre-school and Primary Education Project*. Abingdon: Routledge.
9. Blank, M., Rose, S. and Berlin, L. (1978) *The Language of Learning: The Preschool Years*. New York: Grune & Stratton.
10. Department for Children, Schools and Families (DCSF) (2006) 'Glossary.' *The Early Years Foundation Stage – Consultation on a Single Quality Framework for Services to Children from Birth to Five*. Retrieved from https://www.education.gov.uk/consultations/downloadableDocs/EYFS_11_Glossary.pdf.
11. Arnold, C. and The Penn Green Team. (2010) *Understanding Schemas and Emotion in Early Childhood*. London: Sage.
12. Department for Education (DfE) (2014) *Statutory Framework for the Early Years Foundation Stage*. Retrieved from www.foundationyears.org.uk/eyfs-statutory-framework, on 20 February 2017.
13. Department for Education (DfE) (2017) *Statutory Framework for the Early Years Foundation Stage*. Retrieved from www.foundationyears.org.uk/files/2017/03/EYFS_STATUTORY_FRAMEWORK_2017.pdf, accessed 17 May 2017.
14. Early Education (2012) *Development Matters in the Early Years Foundation Stage*. London: Early Education.
15. Dunphy, E. (2008) *Supporting Early Learning and Development through Formative Assessment. A Research Paper*. Dublin: National Council for Curriculum and Assessment (NCCA). Retrieved from www.ncca.ie/en/Curriculum_and_Assessment/Early_Childhood_and_Primary_Education/Early_Childhood_Education/How_Aistear_was_developed/Research_Papers/Formative_assessment_full_paper.pdf, on 20 February 2017.

Chapter 1

Early Brain Development and How We Learn

CHAPTER OBJECTIVE

This chapter will draw on our understanding of how young children learn and how repeated experiences, such as schematic behaviour, reinforce synapses.

Early brain development

Over recent years scientists have been finding out more and more about how the brain is formed and how it works. This is a fascinating topic and understanding how learning takes place enhances how we engage with very young children. This chapter will draw upon information about how our brains work and link it to schemas and learning.

The brain begins to develop very early in the womb at around three-and-a-half to four weeks when the unborn child develops the *neural plate* and the three main parts of the brain (forebrain, midbrain and hindbrain). After nine weeks, the unborn child's brain has all its major structures in place, and can now begin to make connections between *neurons*, or brain cells. From this early stage, the brain controls reflexes such as the baby's heartbeat, breathing, swallowing, sucking, and blood pressure. Although genes begin the process of brain development, it is the early environment and experiences of the child that now start to take over this process.

There has been a lot of debate about nature–nurture and whether we are born with certain dispositions and attitudes (nature) or whether we learn them as we grow and develop (nurture). We are born with certain genes that will affect us, for example, the colour of our eyes or skin. These things are inherited from our biological parents. However, our personality, attitudes and how we learn will depend largely on the things that we experience, the opportunities that we have and the environment in which we live. It is my view that both nature and nurture combine to develop us into the adults we become.

Certainly in terms of how our brain develops, it is sensory experiences that trigger the electrical activity necessary to enable the brain to develop connections and grow. These connections are called *synapses*.

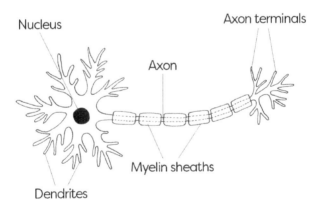

Figure 1.1 A neuron

We are born with a huge number of neurons; some estimates say well over 100 billion, which is more than the number of stars in the Milky Way. Each neuron has a long tentacle-like fibre called an *axon*. The neuron uses the axon to send messages to other neurons. The messages are sent as electrical signals and picked up by thousands of short, hair-like fibres called *dendrites* on other neurons. Each neuron has an axon and dendrites, so it can give and receive messages and is able to communicate with thousands of other neurons. Repeated experiences cause the connections to become well-worn pathways, and the repetition of an action or experience helps to etch these pathways into the brain. Once they have become strengthened sufficiently, they become permanent.

So let's think a little bit about how neurons communicate with each other and how synapses are formed. I like to imagine that someone has walked through a grassy field that no one has walked through before. A pathway is made – we can see where the footsteps have pressed down the grass – but the pathway from A to B is not permanent. If we were to walk along that pathway through the field again and again, eventually the grass would disappear and a clear muddy path would emerge. Through repetition, this path would become permanent.

Using the term 'connection' for these pathways is technically a little misleading, because the neurons do not physically touch each other. There is a tiny gap that remains, across which the information can be shared through electrical impulses. This is usually referred to as a *synaptic gap*. Each neuron can potentially connect to thousands of other neurons, so our brains are made up of a huge network of synapses and neurons, like a dense forest of connections.

As information passes along the axon, a fatty substance called myelin builds up around the axon which acts like insulation allowing the information to transmit faster and more efficiently. The process of building up myelin is called *myelination* and occurs from the third trimester in the womb until adolescence, although myelin grows most rapidly within the early years. When we experience something from a very early age, myelin will grow and the more an experience is repeated, the more myelin a neuron produces. So repeated experiences not only allow the pathways in the brain to become stronger, but they also allow the brain to process information faster. Take, for example, a musician who needs to practise again and again to fine tune their skills until the process of playing a piece of music becomes internalised and they have gained mastery of their craft.[1]

Let's think about what this means in terms of young children. It's that moment when Sarah, a happy two-year-old, brings her key person the same book that she has already read many times that day and wants her key person to read it again! They groan, roll their eyes and try to direct her to a different book. But actually, reading the same book again is exactly what Sarah's brain needs to make those connections and forge those links. She is learning through repeated experiences.

Or Charlie, the 18-month-old who drops his cup again and again and plays that game where we pick up the cup and give it back whereupon he immediately throws it to the floor again! (See Chapter 15.) This repeated behaviour, this trajectory schema (see Chapter 12), is actually all about learning. He is learning through repeated experiences.

It is also about Amiya who loves to sing and dance and requests the 'turtle song' again. It has been sung several times already during the session and the adults are beginning to find it tedious, but she is determined to sing it for the nth time! She is learning through repeated experiences.

And it is also about Naresh (15 months) who is repeatedly taking rings off and putting them onto a post. He is thinking about which ring will fit next and using hand–eye coordination to manipulate the rings into the correct position to place them on the post. This play is schematic (see Chapter 8) and he is learning. He is learning through repeated experiences.

So the process of making connections is strengthened by repetition. Repetition helps the brain carry out its functions and is a foundation of learning, allowing more synapses to be formed and myelination to take place – repetition is how humans are hard-wired to learn.

Synapses are formed most rapidly within the first three years of life and it is during this stage that the brain is ready to learn many things that we take for granted. Young children learn to walk and talk in this phase and the brain has various 'windows of opportunity', as they are sometimes called, when it is primed to form new synapses and develop in certain ways. For example, for language it is generally accepted that the most sensitive period for learning is between the ages of one and three years old, which makes sense to me, since most children will learn to talk in this timeframe. Of course this does not mean that children (and adults) cannot learn outside of these so-called windows. Learning is a lifelong activity, with the brain potentially making connections until the day we die, although some theorists have noted that learning outside of the opportune times becomes more difficult and slower.[2, 3]

The more we repeat an experience, practise a skill or do a particular action, the easier it becomes, until, for some experiences, we manage to complete the task automatically. If we think about our journey to work or a very familiar place, we travel this way so frequently that occasionally we can arrive and not actually remember the journey – it's as if we were on autopilot! Then think about travelling to a new place – our brain will have to work much harder... We may need to get directions, write them down or print them and then pay extra attention to road signs or listen to our Sat Nav along the way. In this case, the neurons involved in navigating to this new destination have not shared synapses frequently before and so they communicate incompletely or inefficiently. This requires forming new connections within the brain, which results in greater conscious effort and attention on our part.

But the story of brain development does not end there. From an early age until late adolescence, the brain begins to prune away some of these connections. Those connections which are not sufficiently strong, have been neglected or are used infrequently are lost. Strong connections are exempt from this process. This is called *synaptic pruning* and the resulting brain has fewer synapses but becomes more powerful as the synapses that remain are much stronger.

Another term that could be misleading is *brain plasticity* or *neuroplasticity*. We tend to use the word plastic to refer to the material used to make many household objects and toys. With regard to the brain, plasticity refers to the brain's ability to reorganise itself, change over time and respond to environmental changes, so it's about the brain being flexible.

No two people will have identical experiences through-out their childhood and it is these individual experiences that piece together our unique character and personality. The pattern of neurons and synapses that remains influences how we think, learn, act and react as adults.

An example of this would be a young child's ability to hear sounds from all languages of the world. During the early years, the brain strengthens connections for sounds in the languages the child hears regularly. Over time, the brain eliminates the connections for other sounds because these sounds are not useful to the child. This is why most adults have trouble distinguishing sounds that are not in their home language. Adults can learn a foreign language, but it may be more difficult than it would be to learn as a child.

How learning takes place

It is important for us to consider how children learn, rather than only thinking about what they are learning. We have already considered the way the brain learns, but for learning to take place, children must have a desire to learn and adopt certain dispositions and attitudes that make a good learner.

In England the EYFS has three characteristics of effective learning which focus on this learning process rather than simply looking at outcomes. These characteristics, 'playing and exploring', 'active learning' and 'creating and thinking critically', are about children's motivation, engagement and thinking.[4] Through maintaining a focus on these and observing children using the characteristics as the lens, practitioners can begin to see the learning taking place more clearly. They could also be used as a tool to help them identify schemas in young children's play.

Other professionals have considered how we learn and share useful ideas, for example, Guy Claxton's Building Learning Power.[5] He has identified four learning capacities:

- resilience – being ready, willing and able to lock on to learning

- resourcefulness – being ready, willing and able to learn in different ways

- reflectiveness – being ready, willing and able to become more strategic about learning

- reciprocity – being ready, willing and able to learn alone and with others.

We could think about schemas in these terms too. Children investigating the world and repeatedly playing in a certain way or showing a fascination for a particular thing are being good learners. They are showing a 'can do' resilient attitude and being resourceful, investigating different ways to do things or finding out why things happen a certain way. They are also sometimes being reflective by thinking about their actions and making links about what they experience: will this happen again if I repeat the action or can I improve on my skills? Children working through a schema may also be happy to learn alone or with others, perhaps sometimes imitating others or collaborating with them to achieve a common goal.

It is widely accepted by theorists and scientists alike that repeated experiences strengthen synaptic development[1] and early experiences shape the brain and children's ability to learn.[6][7][8] As schemas are repeated patterns of behaviour, every time a child is engaged in schematic play, they are actually strengthening the process of learning as their brain makes more connections and becomes more efficient. Grenier[9] states that schema theory 'has the virtue of creating a positive and supportive emotional climate around children's explorations; children are seen as capable, strong and determined, rather than as infuriating and repetitive'.

Observing children in schematic play really highlights that children are 'capable, strong and determined' because it shines a light on what they can do and is a long way removed from the deficit model, which advocates that children begin with very little or no knowledge and thus need to be taught the things they cannot do. As Louis[10] reminds us, 'schema theory is concerned with what children can do, rather than what they cannot do'. This positive stance begins with practitioners who observe children and attune themselves to children's interests and fascinations.

References

1. McNeil, F. (2009) *Learning with the Brain in Mind*. London: Sage.
2. Sousa, D. (2016) *How the Brain Learns*. Thousand Oaks, CA: Corwin Press.
3. Bentzen, M, and Hart, S. (2015) *Through Windows of Opportunity*. London: Karnac Books.
4. Department for Education (DfE) (2014) *Statutory Framework for the Early Years Foundation Stage*. Retrieved from www.foundationyears.org.uk/eyfs-statutory-framework, on 21 February 2017.
5. Claxton, G. (2002) *Building Learning Power*. Bristol: TLO Limited.
6. Atherton, F. and Nutbrown, C. (2013) *Understanding Schemas and Young Children from Birth to Three*. London: Sage.
7. Gopnik, A. (2010) 'How babies think.' *Scientific American* 303, 1, 76–81.
8. Vygotsky, L. (1978) *Mind in Society: The Development of Higher Psychological Processes*. Boston, MA: Harvard University.
9. Grenier, J. (2014) 'Understanding schemas and young children from birth to three and young children learning through schemas: Deepening the dialogue about learning in the home and in the nursery.' *Early Years* 34, 4, 437–439.
10. Louis, S. (2013) *Schemas and the Characteristics of Effective Learning* (p.7). London: Early Education.

Chapter 2

Observing Young Children

CHAPTER OBJECTIVE

This chapter will share general principles of observation and some practical hints and tips. It will offer advice about the most likely times when schemas will be observed and explain to the reader that a child may explore more than one schema at a time.

Observation is a key strategy used to assess children's development and learning in all quality early years settings. Parents are observing their children too, although they may not refer to it in this way. Observation describes the process of closely watching the children in our care, listening to them and taking note of what we see and hear in terms of their actions, expressions, behaviour and language. It is essential that we take time to evaluate what we have seen or heard, so we can make decisions about the next stages of learning for individuals or groups of children.

Some observations will be planned but some may be a spontaneous capture of an important moment. Practitioners in settings usually link what they have observed with their curriculum or their understanding of child development. It is likely that observations of everyday activities will provide evidence of engagement in more than one area of learning or subject.

Mud play observation

Katherine and Rachel were in the outside area playing with the mud kitchen. They were talking about making cakes. Katherine had mixed some soil and water in a large bowl and spooned it into the individual bun sections of the baking tray.

Katherine: 'I'm making some cakes.'

Rachel: 'I am too. I'm making a cake for my mummy.' She sprinkled some grass onto her mud mixture.

Katherine picked up a fork and stirred the mixture in the bun tray and said, 'Icky, sticky, icky, sticky.'

Rachel: 'Icky, sticky, ooh.'

Both girls giggled and Rachel picked up a whisk to stir the grass into her mud cake mixture. 'Round and round you go mud!'

Katherine: 'It's not mud, it's actually cake mix anyway!'

Rachel: 'Yes, I'm stirring it all up to make a cake for my mummy.'

These children are learning about solids and liquids and changing properties of materials, which could indicate a transforming schema (see Chapter 13). They are questioning what happens when they add more water or more grass. They are thinking critically about maths and capacity: what if I pour this into that container? Will it fit? What will happen if it doesn't? They are developing their fine and gross motor skills, stirring, mixing and spooning the mud. They are using lovely descriptive language: 'Icky sticky, ooh'. Their brains are making connections about why things happen and how the world works, and there are also connections with other people, social interaction and cooperation as the girls interact with each other and share this experience. Is this observation about the children's physical development, language development, mathematical understanding or social development? I believe it is about all of them. We cannot always compartmentalise learning and shouldn't need to! These children are displaying the characteristics of effective learning mentioned in Chapter 1. We can really imagine the engagement and motivation that these children have. This is learning made visible.

According to Cathy Nutbrown, a couple of factors are essential for quality practice in relation to schemas. First, having practitioners who are skilled observers of young children and second, that they can use these observations to plan an interesting, inviting and stimulating learning environment.[1]

Quality practice in terms of observing children is more than just simply watching them. Practitioners need to be analysing what children say and do as a means to try to understand their thinking and actions. We observe children in their play (observation), analyse and interpret our observations (assessment), and use this information to implement future learning opportunities for children (planning). This general cycle of Observation, Assessment and Planning is sometimes referred to as the *Planning cycle* or *OAP cycle*.

Planning or OAP cycle

1. **Observation** – what did we see, hear, notice, observe?

2. **Assessment (analysis and interpretation)** – what does this tell me about the child? What opportunities should we plan for this child? What changes should we make to our provision? Do we need to observe this more? Who do we share this information with?

3. **Planning (implementation)** – carrying out actions, for example, sharing information with parents/carers, planning a specific activity or changing an aspect of our routine or provision.

These observations should not take us away from the children for any length of time. When we interact with children we are the most important resource a child can have.

When we are observing children we are:

- **listening** to children, in terms of what they say and how they say it

- **watching** their interactions with the environment, resources, adults and children

- **linking** what we observe with our knowledge of child development

- **thinking** about what we see and the way the child is learning

- **questioning** children to clarify our observations

- **recording** children's actions and words

- **planning** future learning opportunities based on our observations.

Quality observations usually record children's language and communication. Frances Atherton[2] describes a child who was containing and enveloping and used terms such as 'inside', 'put this into there', 'in the kettle' and 'in car' to accompany his play. Tuning into language and recognising the links between actions and words is an important skill which Chris Athey describes as an 'attuned match' of language and action.[3] In the observation of Katherine and Rachel above, Rachel began to stir her mixture with a whisk and said, 'Round and round you go mud'. This language could indicate an interest in rotation (see Chapter 11); she may be interested in exploring other things that rotate or additional ways of moving objects in a circle.

Practitioners also need to be aware of children's questions and to be ready to ask them questions, in addition to reciprocating in their use of schematic language. This 'co-thinking' respects children's thoughts and ideas and can help to demonstrate that the adult values what the child is doing and saying.[4]

What should I observe and note?

Adults who care for young children are observing children all the time, although we may not always record these observations. In terms of recording observations as early years practitioners, we should be on the lookout for significant achievements or, as I like to call them, WOW moments! These are seen when a child:

- attempts something new or not previously observed

- does something that they have not been able to do before

- surprises us with their knowledge or ability

- applies new knowledge, understanding and skills in a different context

- cooperates or collaborates with others in a new way

- perseveres for longer or overcomes setbacks

- explains something in their own words to an adult or another child

- demonstrates their interest or fascination in a particular action or thing.

Within early years settings, practitioners often engage in additional observation methods for specific purposes. For example, to investigate a specific behaviour of a child or to help them to plan for a child with additional needs, practitioners can use *ABC* or *STAR analysis*. The purpose of some observations is to track a child throughout a session to see which activities they engage with and for how long or to assess how a certain area of provision is used and which children use it, for example observing the book corner, monitoring favourite books and noting children who prefer to spend time in this area.

When we observe young children, we can also identify schemas and schematic behaviour in children's play.

Emily tipped the instruments out of the basket, climbed in and sat down. She then picked up the bells and slipped her arms through them like bracelets. Emily shook her arms and laughed, listening to the bells jingling.

From this observation we could identify an interest in making music and plan lots of opportunities for Emily to play with bells and other instruments. However, if we look more closely at what she is doing, we may also pick up on a possible interest in containing (see Chapter 4) as she has deliberately emptied the box and then climbed into it herself. We can also identify a possible interest in the going through a boundary schema (see Chapter 8) as Emily has placed the bells on her wrists like bracelets. She might have been interested in how her hands move through the ring as the bells slip onto her wrists. It is only through close and careful observation that we can note these subtle fascinations. We would want to observe more to see if she is also interested in containing or going through a boundary in other contexts.

Arnold suggests that we should dig deeper in order to reveal any underlying schematic interests, because tapping into these schemas will provide a more meaningful and appropriate extension for the child.[5] When adults use information about schemas to extend children's learning, they tap into children's fascinations in a deeper and wider context than simply tapping into children's interests. For example, if a child loves trains, we can use this interest and plan future learning opportunities for them; however, if we also identify the connecting schema, we can broaden their learning experience by including this.

Recording observations and documenting learning

Recording our observations and using them to support future learning can be called documentation of learning.

Basically, recording and documenting means writing things down. There are many reasons why documenting learning is a good idea. Documentation:

- makes learning visible

- provides a valuable record for parents/carers

- can provide parents with ideas of how to support their child at home

- helps us to demonstrate children's progress

- provides evidence for external advisers/inspectors

- informs practitioners about children's learning and helps them to get to know the children well

- enables practitioners to plan effectively for individual needs

- provides the practitioner with opportunities for reflection and sharing with others

- enables practitioners to talk confidently to parents about their children

- provides evidence that can assist with the early identification of Special Educational Needs and Disabilities (SEND)

- provides communication and language evidence for a child whose first language is not English

- can be easily adapted to meet changing demands of the early years sector.

We can record our observations in many ways. Many practitioners and parents/carers take photographs to record what they see the child doing. In an early years setting, a photograph on its own does not fully explain what is happening.

In this photograph Aisha is riding on a toy motorbike. The photograph acts as a visual prompt and reminds anyone who was there what she was doing on that day. However, what it doesn't do is show the viewer what she was learning through this play. See the two 'Observing learning' examples below.

Observing learning: Example 1

Aisha (14 months) walked over to the toy motorbike, climbed on and rode it in the outside play area.

Observing learning: Example 2

Aisha (14 months) toddled over to the toy motorbike. She stood, a little unsteadily, holding onto the bike with both hands, then lifted her right leg up in an attempt to climb onto the motorbike. The motorbike rolled slightly forwards. Aisha moved forwards and tried again to get her leg over the motorbike. Again, the motorbike rolled forwards and she toddled after it. After several attempts,

Aisha managed to get her leg over the motorbike and sat down on the seat. She then used both legs to push herself forwards.

We could include a caption for the photograph like the text in Example 1 to build on the image that the photograph is providing; however, this does not include any indication of what she was learning. In Example 2, the narration expands our understanding of what Aisha was doing and makes the learning visible. We have a fuller picture of how she came to be on the motorbike and the amount of perseverance and effort that was required on her part. This observation describes Aisha demonstrating the characteristics of effective learning. She is willing to have a go and showing a 'can do' attitude (playing and exploring), she is maintaining focus for a sustained period of time, persisting with an activity when challenges occurred (active learning) and problem solving (creating and thinking critically).

We can include children in recording and documenting learning. Article 12 of the United Nations Convention on the Rights of the Child[6] states that all children have the right to say what they think and be listened to by adults when they make decisions that affect them. Involving children in recording and documenting their own learning can help us to listen to children and involve them in the decisions that affect them.

Kate is a childminder working with three children under four years old and two children who attend school. Kate has developed a scrapbook in which she collects annotated photographs, anecdotal observations of children and children's creations and mark-making. She plans next steps for children based on what they can do and how she feels she can support and extend their interests and abilities. Kate also tries to involve children in the process of recording and documenting. They often help to stick the photos into the scrapbooks and she asks the children to reflect upon what they were learning in the picture. She has developed a system of speech bubbles which she sticks into their books and captures their language and phrases verbatim. Kate also gave the camera to the children so that they could take photographs of the parts of her setting that they liked best.

She was able to discuss the photos with the children, asking why they liked this particular area and use this information to plan future learning opportunities. For example, one of Kate's children took this photo of the outside area and told Kate that they preferred playing outside. Kate was able to amend her provision and plan additional opportunities for this child to learn outside.

Documentation enables children to:

- reflect on their own learning
- be involved in collating the information
- feel valued and increase their self-esteem

- use recall and memory skills
- think about the learning that took place
- instruct practitioners on what to record ('What do you want me to write?')
- develop their use of language
- be involved in decisions that affect them
- have a voice about the provision that they attend.

Many early years settings in England are choosing to record observations using technology and software packages designed to collate this information. If we find this approach helpful and meaningful to our specific children and families, then it can be a useful way of recording information. Much of society is moving to a paperless system and early years settings may wish to follow this path. My advice for practitioners who record and document learning using technological systems is twofold. First, we must ensure that we do not spend too much time interacting with children from behind a screen. Children live in a society where many adults they meet will have their faces buried in a screen of some sort and we need our settings to counter this trend, to provide children with examples of real interaction and an alternative way to communicate. Second, ensure that any observations are backed up regularly and check that any parents who do not have access to a computer can still see their child's profile or learning record.

Other settings choose to record observations by collating them in a file or book as a learning story or learning journal. These systems usually contain information about the child, annotated photographs and narrations which demonstrate learning and development. This sort of record can also contain samples of children's creations or notes that they have written. It is easy to demonstrate progress that children are making with this sort of system, particularly if they are collated in chronological order.

Methods of documenting

- Learning diaries/scrapbooks/portfolios/ring-binder with section for each child or learning area

- Anecdotal observations (WOW moments)

- Focused child observations or key person observations

- Creations (cuttings, drawings, paintings)

- Annotated photographs (of children engaged in activities or of their work)

- Examples of mark-making and writing – child-initiated = best!

- Next steps for children – aids planning and demonstrates progress

- Child conferencing notes/parent comments

- Daily diaries

- Whole group/class documentation of projects

- Notes made by practitioners on planning sheets (evaluations or comments)

- Technological systems of recording learning

It is vital that early years settings, practitioners and parents/carers work closely together and build up trusting relationships. Parents/carers will often be given the documentation when their child leaves the setting, which acts as a lovely record of their time with us and a memory to treasure for children and their families. When a setting documents children's learning by recording their observations of a child, and shares this information with parents and carers, they:

- provide opportunities for parents/carers to see what goes on during a session
- provide an insight into the child's morning: 'I played...'
- reassure parents/carers that 'in five minutes they were fine...'
- show parents/carers evidence of friendships
- give parents/carers something to talk about with their children
- provide a lovely record that parents/carers will treasure
- enable parents and carers to work on the children's next steps at home, which contributes to continuity between home and setting
- build a positive partnership between home and setting.

Using information gathered through observations

When we analyse and interpret our observations, we are assessing what children can do. There are two main types of assessment within the early years: *summative assessment* and *formative assessment*. It is the latter that is generally considered to be effective in the early years, since it informs our practice and can also be called observational assessment. Summative assessment is a snapshot of learning at a particular time. Developmental tick-lists, exams and tests are all examples of summative assessment. Two children could look identical when assessing children in this way, whereas in reality they are very different in terms of their learning needs.

When we use and record our observations we have evidence of children's progress over time and gain insights into children's learning, development and needs. We then must act on this information. This is formative assessment in practice. It describes the process of observing children and using the information to plan next steps in their learning and development. Next steps can be called different things (e.g. areas to develop, targets or future learning opportunities), but it's all about using what we know about the child to plan different activities and experiences for the future. When we do this, we are deciding where they need to go in their future learning, their next step.

Key question to help plan next steps

- What do my observations tell me about the child's learning and development?

- What have I found out that is new or something I haven't observed before?

- Have I observed any fascinations or schematic behaviour?

- What opportunities should I plan for this child?

- What changes (if any) should I make to our provision?

- Do I need to observe this more?

- Who do I share this information with?

Using our observations and acting on the information, could also include:

- **Identifying a schema or schematic behaviour** and planning future opportunities based around this interest, e.g., we identify an interest in containing and offer access to lots of different containers, boxes and baskets and plenty of objects to contain.

- **Tapping into a child's interests** and planning a specific activity that will interest them, e.g., child has a pet dog and has talked about how he took Benji to the dog doctor. We may decide to set up a role play scenario as a vets, or visit our local vet or pet centre.

- **Changing routines** to support the needs of a child, e.g., during late morning snack time, our new two-year-old seems very tired and clingy. We change our routine to have an earlier snack followed by quiet time, when everyone settles down for half an hour to sleep, read or play quietly indoors, rather than move straight from snack to another busy activity or experience.

- **Planning activities to extend and support learning and development**, e.g., we observe that a younger child in our care is very interested in rotation. We decide to provide additional resources and materials to encourage this schema, such as different-sized balls and wheels.

- **Sharing with parent/carer what you have observed**, e.g., a child is exhausted on Thursday mornings and doesn't seem her usual self on this day. We share with her parent and find out that every Wednesday evening she spends time with her father and older siblings and has a much later night than she would usually have. We can then adapt our provision in the light of this new information.

- **Sharing what you have observed with an outside agency.** We may occasionally be concerned about our observations and want to share this with an outside agency – whenever possible, we must seek parental permission for this, unless we believe that it is a safeguarding issue and in doing so the child would be put at further risk. We may be concerned about the development of a child's speech and language and encourage the parent/carer to talk to their health visitor or refer the child to a specific service.

There must be an element of reflection upon what is being observed, and as Cathy Nutbrown[7] suggests, practitioners need to 'watch with open eyes and keep open minds about the meaning and importance of what they see'. This implies that practitioners need to be objective about their observations and try not to make assumptions about what children are hoping to achieve or might be thinking. It necessitates a thorough dissection of the actions and behaviour, as the adult seeks to find patterns and make links. The adult becomes the great detective, unpicking the scene and searching for meaning in the mystery of the child's unfathomable behaviour. It also requires practitioners to have open ears as children may provide us with clues about their schemas in what they say. Creating this sort of environment and climate does not happen by chance. Rather it is through the careful observation of behaviour and fine attunement to children's interests and fascinations.

References

1. Nutbrown, C. (2011) *Threads of Thinking* (4th ed.). London: Sage.
2. Atherton, F. and Nutbrown, C. (2013) *Understanding Schemas and Young Children from Birth to Three*, pp.38–39. London: Sage.
3. Athey, C. (2007) *Extending Thought in Young Children: A Parent–Teacher Partnership* (2nd ed.). London: Sage.
4. Louis, S., Beswick, C., Magraw, L. and Hayes, L. (2013) *Understanding Schemas in Young Children. Again! Again!* London: Bloomsbury.
5. Arnold, C. and The Penn Green Team. (2010) *Understanding Schemas and Emotion in Early Childhood*. London: Sage.
6. Unicef (1989) *A Summary of the* UN Convention on the Rights of the Child (UNCRC). Retrieved from https://downloads.unicef.org.uk/wp-content/uploads/2010/05/UNCRC_summary.pdf, on 14 March 2017.
7. Nutbrown, C. (2011) *Threads of Thinking* (4th ed.), p.157. London: Sage.

SCHEMAS

Chapter 3

Connecting

CHAPTER OBJECTIVE

This chapter will explore observations relating to children who like to join or connect materials or objects together. It will also talk about a 'disconnecting' schema. It will offer ideas of how to extend this play in terms of activities and resources.

What? Observing the connection schema

Connections and disconnections are all around us, from a simple task like dressing, with all the many different fastenings, to a more complicated task like assembling a flat-packed piece of furniture. Some children can become particularly interested in how objects and materials join together. This is described as a connecting schema.

Jack (19 months) is playing making a fence for the farm animals and joining the pieces together. He concentrates very hard joining all the pieces. His key person asks if he needs some help to connect them and he says, 'No, I do it!' Jack then disconnects the fence and joins it again. He repeats this again and again and does not appear interested in enclosing any animals inside the fence.

Georgia (17 months) is playing with the wooden train track and focusing hard on connecting two pieces of track together. After a couple of minutes of trying, she is successful and then gets a train and moves it over the short piece of track. She tries to join more pieces of track together and spends a further five minutes joining another piece on. She is very pleased with the end result, smiles and claps her effort!

Juliette (5 years 6 months) enjoys knotting things together at every opportunity. Once, she tied the lead of her toy dog onto her pushchair and another time she created an elaborate high wire with her dressing gown cord, tying it onto her door handle and bed frame. She then hung a couple of coat hangers onto the cord and moved them along like a zip wire.

Noah (3 years 8 months) is very imaginative and loves to engage in arts and crafts projects on the making table. He spends a long time using different collage materials and cutting them up and sticking them together with glue. Sometimes Noah describes what he is making as an invention and will use glue and sticky tape to join pieces together. His inventions usually involve layers and layers of different pieces of paper all stuck on top of each other like a paper tower.

During a *forest school* session Tom (4 years 10 months) collected sticks and made a long line of them. He made sure that the ends of each stick were touching each other and positioned them accurately and carefully. He continued with this play for most of the session.

The connection schema can be observed in all ages of children and usually involves children focusing on joining pieces together, either by attaching them in some way or making them physically touch each other.

We may see children:

- choosing to play with train track and enjoying putting together the track

- placing toys so that they touch each other in some way

- gluing and sticking different materials together

- fastening things together
- threading beads, etc. to make long strings or necklaces
- enjoying disconnecting train track
- building chains out of objects
- positioning toys so that the ends all touch each other
- lining up sticks or leaves end to end, ensuring that they touch in a long line
- tying things up using rope
- tying toys together using ribbon, string or knotting material
- taking things apart
- playing with jigsaws
- knocking down towers repeatedly.

So what? Interpreting the connection schema

Children who have a connection schema are particularly interested in connecting things together, disconnecting things or making toys and materials touch and join in some way. Jack is independently joining the fence pieces for the farm. He concentrates on this task for a long time and refuses any help offered, determined to complete this task himself. He is improving his manual dexterity and fine motor skills while attaching one edge of the fence to another. The fence has concave and convex parts which need to be perfectly aligned before it will fit together. Jack completes this intricate task independently and shows little interest in enclosing any animals inside the fencing. His fascination is with connecting and disconnecting the pieces of fence.

In a similar way Georgia concentrates really hard on joining the train track together. This is a slightly simpler task than the fence as it fits together like a loose jigsaw piece, yet it still requires good fine motor control and a lot of concentration. She focuses on this task, joining more pieces of track together until she feels that she has enough for her train. Her pleasure and satisfaction in achieving the task of connecting the track is wonderful to see as she gives herself a clap!

Juliette is particularly interested in connecting things together using ropes, cords and string. She is thinking about how to fasten things together using knots and explores this at every opportunity. The way that she uses the dressing gown cord as a sort of zip wire could indicate that she is also exploring how things move along a rope or line and linking connection with movement.

Noah appears to love the process of attaching things together rather than the end product of what he is creating. The way that he layers paper and other materials on top of each other, indicates that he is particularly interested in connecting them together. A child like Noah will enjoy using different types of glue and sticky tape to join materials and will usually spend a long time creating at a making table.

Tom demonstrated his interest in a connection schema through lining up the sticks and making the ends touch each other. It would be interesting to observe whether or not he also has a positioning schema and is interested in the position of objects. Tom is thinking about how the ends of the sticks connect with each other. Does this large stick reach the smaller one? Can 1 position them so that they touch constantly? Would a different stick fit better?

What next? Extending the connection schema

We can extend the connection schema and support children in many different ways. For example, we could provide Jack some different types of construction materials that attach in different ways; this could challenge his fine motor skills. He will probably want to use the materials himself, so we could play alongside Jack, modelling how to connect the pieces without directly teaching him. Georgia may also like to explore different ways of connecting things – perhaps she would be interested in threading or using something that has one way of connecting. This would be a more difficult task than joining the track and she may enjoy the satisfaction of achieving something difficult.

Juliette is particularly fascinated with using rope and tying knots, and her parents and carers would need to be aware of this in order to supervise her play, without putting too many limits in place. It is important to remember not to provide lengths of rope, string or ribbon for young children to use without adequate supervision. Children can become entangled in relatively short lengths of cord with potentially devastating consequences. We can incorporate Juliette's interests into new learning opportunities by offering her different lengths and thicknesses of ropes and ribbons. She may want to explore this different aspect of connection. She may also enjoy playing on a zip wire, so if we are able to, we could take her to a local park that has a zip wire or similar for her to play on.

We can extend Noah's thinking by offering him different types of fastening and a greater variety of things to attach. Noah has enjoyed using glue and sticky tape in the past; perhaps he would like to experiment with paperclips, treasury tags or different types of sticky tape, like masking tape, for a new experience enabling him to connect things in different ways.

We might want to support Tom to explore further using sticks by encouraging him to collect sticks and even logs of different lengths and diameters. Do different-sized sticks fit together in the same way? One of the advantages to being outside is that children like Tom can explore and investigate on a large scale, so perhaps Tom will want to join in a competition to see who can make the longest line? Or maybe we can attach some string and actually tie the sticks together?

If we recognise the connection schema in any of our children, we can provide additional resources and activities to support and extend their thinking. Here are some suggestions showing how we can support children who show a fascination for connection:

- Make chains with the children out of daisies, paper, pipe-cleaners or paperclips.

- Build spiders' webs with thread and sticks.

- Encourage children to weave or thread leaves onto a stick.

- Provide string and rope and toys and objects that can tie together, e.g., skipping ropes (ensure that this activity is supervised).

- Offer opportunities to build a train track, road or fences.

- Provide a range of construction materials that join and connect in different ways.

- Provide tubes, pipes and guttering outside for large-scale connection projects.

- Offer access to magnetic toys and construction materials.

- Ensure that our dressing-up clothes have a range of different fastenings.

- Provide pipes and funnels in sand and water play to make connections.

- Offer sticky tape, masking tape, gloopy glue, glue sticks, paperclips, treasury tags, rubber bands, etc. for junk modelling.

- Offer access to hole punches so that children can thread paper together to make mobiles.

- Offer materials for threading, e.g., pasta, beads, cotton reels, ribbon or shoe laces.

- Play games that involve children holding hands and connecting, e.g., circle games.

- Provide chunky chalks so that children can draw lines outside from one area to another.

- Offer children a variety of jigsaws with a different number of pieces and that connect in different ways.

- Use words to support this schema, such as connect, join, fasten, together, apart, separate, construct, build, disconnect, knot, through, thread, in, on top.

Links with other schemas

The connection schema links very closely with the positioning schema (see Chapter 10) as children are usually concerned about the position of an object or toy. This is clearly seen with Tom positioning the sticks in a long line.

Children may also be particularly interested in the going through a boundary schema (Chapter 8) and particularly enjoy threading, weaving or sewing activities to support and extend both schemas. Noah may be interested in sewing as he is particularly interested in creating things. Juliette may enjoy threading and weaving as alternative ways to use string, wool and cord.

Some children can also become fascinated with disconnecting things, which could appear to be mis-behaviour (e.g., taking things apart), but interpreting this behaviour from a schematic perspective can shed new light onto the children's thoughts, actions and behaviour. In Chapter 15 we meet Jack again, and observe him knocking down towers, which links the connection schema with a trajectory movement.

Chapter 4

Containing

CHAPTER OBJECTIVE

This chapter will share observations of children who repeatedly fill and empty containers and/or bags. It will offer ideas of how to extend this play in terms of activities and resources.

What? Observing the containing schema

Containing things is part and parcel of our everyday lives. We take bags shopping, use a laundry basket for clothes, put things in our pockets, carry a handbag or purse, tidy things away into baskets; and many of us love to invest in containers and ornamental boxes to keep jewellery and odds and ends in. Imitation is one of the main ways that very young children learn, so perhaps it is not surprising that the containing schema appears to be observed more frequently than others. Often children become fascinated with putting things into and taking things out of bags. It is also amusing that children around the world, when given a large toy to unwrap, are often more fascinated with the large box it came in than the gift! Many children enjoy putting things inside other things, including themselves. This schema can also include containing themselves in boxes or containers.

Katie (3 years 10 months) walks across the nursery pushing the doll's pushchair. She has loaded it up with several bags which she spent time filling with various bits and pieces. She moves to the small world area and fills up the pushchair seat with people and cars. Her mum has shared that Katie has always had an interest in bags. When she was younger she would empty out the contents of her mum's handbag onto the floor, much to her mum's annoyance!

Isaac (4 years 8 months) usually has four or five stones in his pocket and his mum has even put stones through the wash! Isaac collects sticks and stones whenever he can and can often be found filling up his dumper truck with various things from the garden.

While on holiday with her parents, Zoe (2 years 4 months) visited the beach. She carried all three buckets at the same time and spent a long time gathering stones and shells to collect in the buckets. Zoe's mum offered to help Zoe carry the buckets and Zoe responded, 'I do it, my buckets!'

Jane (2 years 10 months) loves to climb into spaces and will frequently be found emptying toys out of a box so that she can climb into it. She will sometimes say, 'I'm in a car!' or 'Look, I'm in a boat!' Jane also puts her teddies into boxes and her mum told the nursery that she has several shoe boxes and baskets in her room which she has filled with her soft toys. She also said that at Christmas and birthdays Jane is more interested in the packaging and boxes than the toy that was in them.

Lydia (2 years 6 months) enjoys sorting toys and materials into different containers. Her childminder provided her with different-coloured bowls and she spent a long time sorting out pom-poms into colours, matching the colour of the bowl to the pom-pom.

We may see children:

- climbing into boxes or containers
- filling containers
- filling their pockets

- filling trucks, transporters, pushchairs, prams, trolleys etc. with toys or resources

- filling buckets with sand, water, gravel, soil, etc.

- plugging sinks to contain the water

- emptying containers (including the tissue box!)

- tipping their toys out of boxes onto the floor

- posting things into spaces, behind radiators, through letterboxes

- using shape sorters or posting toys

- filling and emptying bags, handbags, rucksacks, suitcases, etc.

- putting toys to bed in cots, shoe boxes or any suitable container.

So what? Interpreting the containing schema

Children interested in putting themselves or different things into some sort of container probably have a containing schema. There is usually at least one 'Katie' in every nursery environment and in many homes around the world – the child, often a girl, who collects odds and ends and keeps them in handbags or bags. In our house, when a jigsaw piece has gone missing or no one can find the magnifying glasses, we tend to search inside the range of handbags and rucksacks that are in our middle daughter's room. It is highly likely to be in one of those bags, as she is very interested in containing.

Through containing, Katie is enjoying the process of putting things in the various bags that she has hung on the pushchair. She is also interested in transporting (see Chapter 14), and these two schemas often go hand in hand. Katie is investigating concepts relating to volume and capacity. How much will fit in this bag? Will this toy squeeze into that backpack? These ideas will also support her in her developing understanding of spatial awareness and size. Katie has shown an interest in emptying her mum's handbag. Emptying is also part of the containing schema. In order to fill something, it sometimes needs to be emptied. When children empty containers, it can be frustrating and viewed as misbehaviour. However, it could simply be further evidence that a child is exploring a containing schema (see Chapter 15 for further information).

Isaac is also exploring these ideas when he fills his pockets and dumper truck to overflowing with sticks and stones. He is enjoying collecting the sticks and stones and might be thinking about other criteria when he selects them, for example, this stone is round and flat so I'll collect this one, that stone is jagged and sharp so I might not collect that one. It would be interesting to ask Isaac if he only collects certain sticks and stones as this may help us to interpret his thinking.

Through the containing schema, Zoe is also exploring her independence and control. She is keen to be in charge of carrying the buckets and putting shells and stones inside them. At two years old, Zoe is pushing her gross motor skills to the limit by attempting to carry several large buckets at once. This is typical behaviour for this age group – they enjoy demonstrating to others that they can do it, and phrases such as 'mine' or 'I do it' are commonplace. They are finding out about their capabilities and exploring what they can and cannot do yet. Zoe is developing her sense of self and who she is. She is taking control of aspects of her life whenever she can.

Jane has a clear interest in containing herself, hence climbing into boxes at every available opportunity. She is thinking about space and capacity – will I fit in there, what does it feel like to be inside that space? She is using her imagination – I could climb into that box and make it a boat or car. Jane also enjoys containing with her soft toys, placing them into shoe boxes and baskets, exploring this same schema from a different perspective.

Lydia is ordering and classifying as she sorts the pom-poms into different colours. She uses the coloured containers to separate the pom-poms and appears to enjoy creating order out of the chaos of the mixed up pom-poms. She is possibly engaged in a containing schema as she places the pom-poms in bowls. It would be interesting to note whether she is engaged in containing objects, or herself, in other areas of play. Does she enjoy filling bags and containers while in the home corner, for example?

What next? Extending the containing schema

We can tap into children's interests in containing by planning future learning opportunities for them. For example, Katie may relish the opportunity to explore different-sized bags. Perhaps she could create a collection of bags of different shapes and sizes and several little things to fill them. This would really capture her interest. Isaac might enjoy going into the outdoor area to collect sticks and stones with an adult who could chat to him about his collection. By collecting sticks and stones alongside Isaac, it would show genuine interest in what he is doing as well as demonstrate that he has permission to do this. Isaac might also like to explore a pebbly beach or read some books relating to dumper trucks and how they transport things in real life.

We could provide Jane with lots of opportunities to contain herself – perhaps offering her a really large box to play inside or access to den-building materials. Lydia may want to investigate different ways of sorting; or if her interest is particularly in colours, she may enjoy sorting some different objects into colours too.

If we recognise the containing schema in any of our children, we can provide additional resources and activities to support and extend their thinking. Here are some suggestions for how we can support children who show a fascination for containing objects or themselves:

- Provide a variety of different objects and containers for children to fill.

- Provide a variety of different objects that can be used to fill containers, e.g., pebbles.

- Ensure that we have an 'ethos of permission' allowing children to fill and empty different containers.

- Provide boxes and containers large enough for children to climb into to contain themselves.

- Ensure that the containers provided are of different shapes and sizes.

- Provide opportunities for burying objects and finding them again in the sand or earth.

- Invest in some shape-sorting toys.

- Provide baskets and natural materials to be sorted into groups, e.g., feathers, pebbles, sticks, leaves, conkers, shells.

- Offer activities that encourage children to classify and sort objects into groups.

- Include containers in different contexts, e.g., with playdough, in the role play area or outside.

- Allow children to play with the pots and pans in the kitchen and put objects into and take objects out of them.

- Encourage children to make dens and hideaways to hide objects and themselves.

- Provide clothes with lots of pockets to fill for children to wear or dress a teddy in clothes with several pockets.

- Offer a selection of handbags, baskets and rucksacks for children to play with.

- Encourage younger children to take control and do things for themselves, e.g., carrying objects or filling containers.

- Offer opportunities to investigate capacity and volume using various containers in sand and water play.

- Provide trucks and lorries, prams and trolleys that children can use as containers.

- Encourage children to join in with tidying up and putting toys away.

- Use language associated with container play: in, out, into, empty, full, space, room, fit, inside, outside.

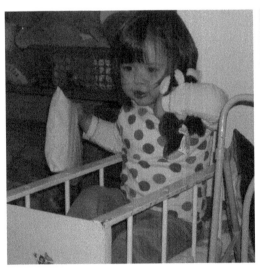 

Links with other schemas

The containing schema is one of the most frequently observed and it links quite closely with other schemas such as transporting (see Chapter 14), enclosing (see Chapter 6) and positioning (see Chapter 10) or connecting (see Chapter 3). For example, Katie enjoyed loading up the pushchair with bags, people and cars and also enjoyed pushing this loaded pushchair around. She was transporting the things she had collected. Whether her main interest was in containing the toys or transporting them around would only really be determined through observation. However, we can easily provide for both schemas for Katie to extend her thinking by offering her lots of opportunities to fill bags and several different options for transporting, for example, trolley, pushchair, large toy truck or doll's pram.

Jane was particularly interested in getting into boxes and this links very closely with the enclosing schema, the desire to make enclosures around self or objects, and the enveloping schema, when children like to hide or be covered up. The best way to find out if Jane is also interested in enclosing and enveloping (see Chapters 6 and 7) is through observing her and reflecting upon the observations.

Lydia is engaged in very ordered play as she organises the pom-poms into different colours. She is making connections between the pom-poms, classifying them as a particular colour in order to place it in the 'correct' bowl, thus linking with the connecting schema. She is also carefully positioning each pom-pom as she shows an interest into where the pom-poms are in terms of each coloured bowl, linking with a possible positioning schema.

Chapter 5

Core and Radial

CHAPTER OBJECTIVE

This chapter will share case studies (including drawings) of children who enjoy combining trajectory and rotation schemas, for example, drawing lines coming out from a core like a sun. It will offer ideas of how to extend this play in terms of activities and resources.

What? Observing the core and radial schema

Core and radial is an interesting schema to observe as it combines the straight movements of trajectory schemas and the circular movements of rotation schemas. The word core here means centre and radial means arranged in lines from a central point. Think about how children typically draw a sun shining. They tend to draw a circle and then add lines or rays sticking outwards, fairly evenly spaced around the circumference of the circle. Or imagine the spokes on a bicycle tyre – this is another typical core and radial image. These 'sun' and 'spokes' shapes can also be found in our daily lives if we imagine how we might cut a pizza or cake, or picture the sun icon being used in various situations, as an emoticon or to indicate sunshine. In addition, any structure where we see a round nut or screw head attaching straight lines or poles depicts this core and radial image.

Some children can become fascinated with drawing and creating these images, either on paper or using various different materials. They may also choose to move their bodies, combining rotating and swinging movements.

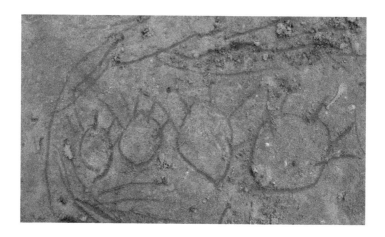

Jayden (3 years 10 months) used a stick to draw shapes in the mud. First he drew circles and said, 'This is a footprint look!' He then added lines to the circles, saying, 'Look, claws, claws! It's a Gruffalo footprint!' Jayden then moved to a new patch of mud and drew more circles and lines and chatted about the Gruffalo footprints he was making.

Tina (5 years) was using the construction materials to create lines going out from a central point. She added straight pieces in turn, working clockwise around the circular piece, and continued making this shape until she had used up all of the available circular pieces as her central points.

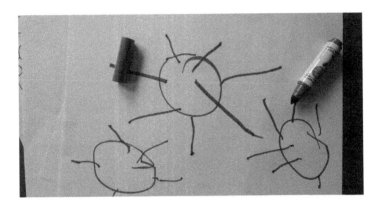

John (4 years 2 months) was sitting in the graphics area at nursery. His key person had noticed that he had previously loved to draw circles or lines but today John drew both lines and circles together to make sun shapes. He told his key person that he had drawn lots of suns.

While she was 'helping' her mummy in the kitchen, Lydia (18 months) made playdough cakes. She then began decorating her cakes with straws and repeatedly fixed them in the dough so that they stuck up out of the dough. Lydia's mummy encouraged this play, saying to Lydia, 'Have we made candles? Are they birthday cakes?' and suggesting that they sing 'Happy Birthday' and count the straw candles together.

The core and radial schema is usually identified when children appear to be interested in both circular and straight movements. We may see children:

- twirling toys then letting go, like 'shot-put' or 'hammer' in athletics
- rolling balls along the ground or along ramps
- drawing circles and lines in their mark-making
- drawing 'suns'
- drawing shapes like bicycle tyres
- creating a construction with many lines protruding from a central point
- unrolling the toilet paper
- making 'birthday cakes' or hedgehogs in playdough or clay
- using rolling pins and rolling playdough or clay
- twisting up a swing and un-winding it while sitting on it
- playing on a tyre swing that rotates as it swings back and forth
- enjoying rides at the fairground that both rotate and move in straight lines
- playing games that involve both straight lines and circular movements, e.g., skittles or swing-ball

- engaging in bubble play, as children may be interested in the roundness of the bubbles combined with their trajectory in the wind – also it's such fun!

So what? Interpreting the core and radial schema

Jayden uses his stick to make shapes that indicate an interest in core and radial. It would be interesting to note whether or not he has shown an interest in trajectory and rotational schemas. We do not know whether Jayden draws the circles already intending them to be footprints or if he looks at the shapes and decides that they could be footprints. By adding lines he relates the way the drawing looks to the Gruffalo.

Tina was particularly interested in making lines protrude out from each circular piece. The construction materials that she had chosen to use lend themselves to core and radial shapes since they allow a circular central piece to connect with several straight lines. However, not all children would automatically make this sort of shape. Tina was methodical in the way that she was attaching the straight lines to the central points; she deliberately made the 'sun' pattern in her play, adding straight pieces one by one to her design. She was like a research scientist methodically constructing every possible arrangement with the available materials.

John is interesting because he has demonstrated an interest in both drawing lines and circles previously in his play. This particular drawing was significant because he was combining his interest in lines and circles and drawing 'suns'. This is fairly typical in terms of children's development of drawing. They begin to make marks in a random scribbling phase, which develops into more controlled marks like lines and circular movements. The circles get more and more advanced as children become more dexterous and their fine motor control increases. Their controlled marks now have meaning as children draw to represent their thoughts and ideas about the world around them. It is in this controlled scribbling phase that children tend to build on their skills of drawing lines and circles by combining them, just like John, making suns and radials.

Cathy Nutbrown[1] said:

> When spiders, spokes and sunshine appear in children's drawings, they have most of the marks they need to write all the symbols in the written scripts of many languages. So the early development of schemas through children's physical movement provides an essential underpinning for eventually beginning to write.

She is describing the shapes that John was drawing, which can be referred to as core and radial, so his exploration of drawing these shapes is supporting his ability to write letters and thus will also help him as he becomes a writer over the next year or so.

Lydia was adding straws to her playdough 'cakes', making shapes that imply a core and radial schema. It would be interesting to note whether she also enjoyed representing these shapes in other ways, or was particularly interested in rolling the dough into balls or lines. Lydia's mummy recognises the shapes as candles on a cake, although we do not know if this is an idea that Lydia thought of and her mummy supported or if her mummy initiated this. However the idea came about, Lydia is linking her construction with the dough to her understanding of the world around her and making a representation of a familiar concept – a birthday cake. This schematic play is allowing Lydia to repeat the rolling and squeezing actions needed to manipulate the dough into cakes and also to repeat the pincer grip and hand–eye coordination required to put the candles in place.

What next? Extending the core and radial schema

There are many ways that we can extend children's learning if we observe the core and radial schema in any child under our care. Jayden may be interested in creating 'Gruffalo footprints' in other contexts, for example, tracing the shape in gloop (cornflour and water) or making a 3D model of the Gruffalo's foot and claws with clay or dough. Tina might be fascinated by using a different type of construction material to make her core and radial shapes or perhaps be interested in using recycled materials to represent these shapes. John's key person could plan for him to link his interest in the sun shapes with movement outside and encourage him to join in an obstacle course which combines rotation with trajectory movements. Lydia's mummy was already extending Lydia's thinking as she linked Lydia's core and radial shapes with birthday cakes and candles. If Lydia demonstrated an interest in this, she might want to plan a mini birthday party for one of Lydia's toys and Lydia could make the cake and candles.

The great thing about extending children's schematic play is that the possibilities are endless. If we link new opportunities and activities into children's fascinations and schemas, we can pick up on any number of possible lines of further enquiry. Here are some suggestions for how we can support children who show an interest in the core and radial schema:

- Engage in cooking activities, particularly those that require us to roll out pastry or dough.

- Invest in some construction materials that allow rods and connectors to join.

- Offer opportunities for children to play with malleable materials such as playdough or clay and provide different materials for them to add, e.g., straws, feathers, matchsticks, lolly sticks.

- Allow children to play on a tyre swing or twist a normal swing up and unwind it again.

- Create obstacle courses involving straight lines and rotation, e.g., tunnels, skipping ropes and hoops.

- Investigate different wheels and bicycle spokes.

- Hang some balls on strings from the ceiling and allow children to spin or swing them.

- Thread beads and cotton reels.

- Play skittles or boules as they combine the ball rolling and rotating with the straight movement.

- Provide opportunities for children to cut up pizza or cake in straight lines or provide pretend food with hook and loop fastenings that allow the cake/pizza to be cut.

- Create mini projects on hedgehogs – find different ways of representing hedgehogs in art/craft.

- Offer opportunities for children to create using different recycled materials, e.g., plastic milk-bottle tops, cartons, boxes, tubes, straws.

Links with other schemas

The core and radial schema clearly links with both the rotation (see Chapter 11) and trajectory (see Chapter 12) schemas as it combines the circular 'core' with the straight 'radial' lines which go out like rays from a central point. Therefore we may find that children who show an interest in core and radial are also fascinated with rotation or trajectory schemas.

The core and radial schema may also link with the connecting schema as children may be interested in connecting central points with lines or rods. They may show this interest in their play with construction or malleable materials. This can clearly be seen in the case study about Tina above. She was particularly interested in joining construction materials together and this could indicate an interest in connecting. The shapes that she was creating indicated her interest in a core and radial pattern.

References

1. Nutbrown, C. (2015) *Schemas and Young Children's Learning*. Sheffield: University of Sheffield. Retrieved from www.sheffield.ac.uk/polopoly_fs/1.441757!/file/Schemas.pdf, on 22 February 2017.

Chapter 6

Enclosing

CHAPTER OBJECTIVE

This chapter will share observations about children who display behaviours such as climbing into boxes, tunnels or pop-up houses (anything where they are enclosed) or children who draw borders around their mark-making. It will offer ideas of how to extend this play in terms of activities and resources.

What? Observing the enclosing schema

The washing basket in our house was rarely used as a washing basket. It has been a pirate ship, a rocket and a school for teddies, amongst other things! More often than not, one of my children would sit in it, enjoying being enclosed in the basket. They sometimes squeezed cushions in with them to surround themselves with comfort! The enclosing schema is about children who surround themselves, parts of their body, objects or space with a border. The enclosures can be any size or shape and made from any materials. This schema has very close links with containing and enveloping and is very difficult to discuss in isolation.

Cora (2 years 9 months) was playing with the toy farm when she built this animal pen. She connected the fence together fairly quickly and then focused her attention on placing the animals inside the enclosure. Later on, Cora took the animals out, saying that they were going to have their dinner and then she put some different animals in the enclosure saying, 'You go in, your turn.'

Tom (4 years 2 months) was building with the small wooden blocks. He created a sort of platform with the blocks, laying them side by side on the table. He then balanced two blocks on the top in a T shape. Tom carefully lined up the blocks in a border putting them down one by one, which totally enclosed his construction. As Tom did this he said, 'One more,' and he placed the last block in place. He then went on to make borders with the blocks around a toy cup and another construction made by his brother which was already on the table.

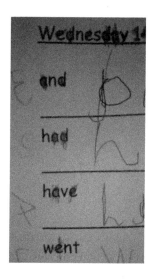

Tina (5 years 4 months) was sitting at a desk in the graphics area. She was writing with a pen, holding it in a pincer grip and carefully colouring in the enclosed spaces in all of the letters that have them, e.g., a, d, e. Her teacher noticed that she also colours in enclosed spaces in numbers, e.g., 0, 4, 6, 8 and 9 and often draws borders around pictures and words.

Carlos (3 years 4 months) was playing with the toy cars on the mat. His key person recognised that he liked playing with the cars and made him a garage out of a shoe box to put the cars into and numbered the spaces in the box. Carlos spent a long time repeatedly moving the cars into and out of the garage spaces. He was talking to himself as he played, saying, 'In you go!' as he 'drove' the cars into the spaces.

Katie (4 years 2 months) loves nothing better than to sit in a box or container. She told her mummy that it is her special space and mummy can't fit into it. Sometimes Katie also fills the box with toys and teddies and climbs in with them. Katie's mum has also shared that Katie surrounds herself with so many toys in her bed at night that sometimes she thinks there won't be room for Katie!

We may see children:

- sitting in boxes
- playing in play tunnels
- enjoying playing in tents or pop-up houses (anything where they are covered)
- drawing borders around their mark-making
- constructing enclosures around themselves
- making enclosures around small world animals or other toys with bricks or other equipment

- joining lines to make enclosures with different materials

- filling enclosures that they have built or made with toys, objects or themselves

- sitting inside a space and surrounding themselves with toys so that they are in an enclosure of toys

- building houses or paddocks with bricks and fences

- appearing fascinated with bracelets, necklaces or watches

- surrounding themselves with cushions

- arranging the food around the edges of their plate

- riding a bike around the perimeter of an area

- colouring in circles or filling in the enclosed spaces in letters e.g. a, b, d, e, g.

So what? Interpreting the enclosing schema

We can tell that Cora was more interested in enclosing the animals than in connecting the fence because of the length of time she committed to each activity. Creating the fence was, for her, a necessary activity in order to get down to the real playing of putting animals inside the space, so she made the fence as quickly as possible and then spent much longer placing the animals in the pen. Cora's language also gives us a clue. She used the phrase 'you go in', which helps to explain the purpose of her play. She was clearly putting the animals into the space and hemming them in with the fence.

Tom focused on making the blocks touch each other, which links with his connecting schema, and he was also positioning the blocks so that they made a T shape – possibly a capital T for Tom. Later he used the blocks to make borders around everything that he could find on the table. Tom says 'one more' as he builds his border, which indicates that he is interested in quantity and he is estimating that he will need another block to finish the enclosure. All of these blocks are the same size as each other so through his constructing he is actually exploring size in terms of units – how many blocks will I need to make a border around the construction? How many will I need around this smaller cup?

Tina is noticing the enclosed spaces in letters and numbers and carefully colours these spaces in. It would be interesting to note if she also showed an interest in enclosing herself in spaces or placing toys in enclosures in her play or containing in any way. Through colouring in the letter spaces she is not only developing her fine motor skills but she is also thinking about holes, spaces and filling them, again with clear links to containing and perhaps enveloping.

Carlos was particularly interested in cars and playing on the car mat. His key person was tapping into this interest to extend his play. Carlos had not picked up on the possibilities to use numbers in his play and through his use of language we can detect his interest in moving the cars into spaces. This links closely with a containing schema (see Chapter 4) and his interest in the position of the cars links with positioning (see Chapter 10). He is exploring the concepts of space and volume.

Katie has a clear interest in enclosing herself in spaces. She sometimes likes to do this alone and occasionally involves her toys in the process. Katie makes it clear to her mum that this is her space and this implies that she is using the box as a way of having a boundary around her, perhaps distancing herself slightly from her mum. Katie also has a clear containing schema and this is evident in how she contains so many toys in her bed at night. She is using her toys to surround herself and perhaps help with a sense of security and safety.

What next? Extending the enclosing schema

We could offer Cora further opportunities to explore the concept of enclosing animals by taking her on a visit to a farm. She might be interested in looking at the different pens and enclosures that they use in the real world. Alternatively, we could offer Cora different opportunities to enclose her animals, e.g., perhaps we could ask if she would like to collect some greenery from the garden to create hedges or small sticks that she can use as a boundary enclosing the space.

By providing Tom access to different materials, perhaps unit blocks or geometric shapes, we could tap into his interest in estimating how many blocks he will need to make borders. He might enjoy the opportunity to make borders out of different materials both inside and outside.

Tina may enjoy the opportunity to fill and empty containers, to enclose herself in spaces or to explore using different media and materials to fill gaps. She could also find activities such as colour by numbers or colouring in intricate patterns satisfying and rewarding.

We can extend Carlos's play further by offering him alternative methods to enclose his cars, perhaps providing a car transporter or tunnel for them to drive through. Carlos might also enjoy creating spaces for the bikes and ride-on cars in the outdoor area, for example, setting up a garage or parking spaces for them. If he begins to show an interest in numbers we could also extend and develop this alongside his interest in enclosing by numbering the parking spaces and bikes.

Katie would relish the opportunity to play with large boxes and containers to put both herself and her toys into. She might enjoy den-making activities and might also like to create her own enclosures for her toys.

We can support and extend the enclosing schema in many ways. Here are some suggestions for children who show an interest in putting themselves or objects into enclosed spaces:

- Offer children access to large pieces of material and clothes horses, or use a washing line to hang the material on – we can secure fabric with pegs or bulldog clips or den/tent building materials.

- Provide big boxes for children to enclose themselves.

- Provide peg boards and pegs.

- Provide resources to make borders on paper.

- Put some paper with borders in the writing/mark-making area.

- Offer houses, garages and car transporters with small world play.

- Provide construction materials that lend themselves to making enclosures, fences, bridges, tunnels, walls and houses.

- Provide lolly sticks, pipe cleaners, ribbon and other materials that children can make borders out of during craft activities.

- Partition the room to create small, enclosed areas.

- Allow children to frame their pictures.

- Offer children opportunities to collect twigs and sticks to make natural borders.

- Provide envelopes for filling and paper for wrapping objects.

- Allow children access to play houses or to play under slides or in other enclosed spaces.

- Collect bandages, bracelets, necklaces, watches and belts which children can use to enclose parts of their bodies.

- Provide play that involves animal enclosures or cages, e.g., vets, farms and zoos.

- Offer opportunities to colour by number/shape.

- Provide stacking toys that fit inside each other, e.g., Russian dolls and cups.

- Play games that involve using the edges of a space, e.g., riding a bike around the perimeter of the garden, moving the a ball around the edge of the parachute.

- Make food that has something inside, e.g., pies, sandwiches, pitta bread pockets.

- Collect segmented boxes, e.g., the insert from a box of chocolates or biscuit tin.

- Provide saris, cloaks and scarves in the role play area.

- Use language such as in, inside, out, around, edge, perimeter, border, fence, enclose, wrap, corner, beside, on top, underneath and contain, to support this schema.

Links with other schemas

The enclosing schema links very closely with other schemas, especially the containing schema (see Chapter 4) and the enveloping schema (see Chapter 7), and it can be difficult to distinguish between them at times. In these schemas children often fill and empty boxes and enclose themselves in spaces or containers. This can clearly be seen in the case studies above about Carlos and Katie as they have a keen interest in putting things and themselves into spaces.

We can also make links with the connecting schema (see Chapter 3) as Tom builds and constructs. In order to create his enclosure, the blocks have to touch each other and he is very specific about where he is placing them, which could also indicate an interest in positioning (see Chapter 10). In addition, Cora may have an interest in the positioning schema as she focuses on the position of the animals, ensuring that they are inside the enclosure of her fence. It would be interesting to observe if she is also interested in the position of other objects in her play. Links to other schemas can only really be identified and confirmed by close observation and attunement to children's interests and fascinations.

Chapter 7

Enveloping

> ## CHAPTER OBJECTIVE
>
> This chapter will share examples of children who like to hide or be covered up, wrap and cover up objects and toys or who dress up in layers of clothing. It will offer ideas of how to extend this play in terms of activities and resources.

What? Observing the enveloping schema

Our youngest child has a very strong enveloping schema. She has always been interested in playing peek-a-boo type games and hiding under covers and blankets. She also loves to wrap up her toys and could often be found using pieces of fabric to wrap teddies and give them to us as 'presents'. In fact, she loved this so much that for her third birthday we gave her an empty cushion cover with a zip so that she could wrap toys to her heart's content!

Laura (2 years 1 month) was hiding in the curtain. She pulled the curtain over her face and waited. Her dad said, 'Where's Laura gone?' and Laura giggled and pulled the curtain back so that he could see her. Her dad responded, 'There you are, Laura!' Laura and her dad repeated this game over and over, both laughing, until Laura's dad lifted Laura onto his knee and began to tickle her.

While at his childminder's house, Naresh (20 months) found this large piece of netting and enjoyed hiding under it. His younger friend Julia (16 months) loved pulling it off his head and Naresh would put it back over his head again. They repeated this over and over while both laughing and really enjoying the turn taking of this game. Naresh said, 'I see you!' and then they swapped roles and Julia hid under the netting while Naresh pulled it off her head.

Hayden (4 years 5 months) was playing in the outside play area pretending to be a pirate. He lay the pirate flag down on the deck of his pirate ship (climbing frame platform) and climbed down saying, 'I need treasure!' He then searched in the outside area for treasure (aka pebbles) and climbed back on board his ship to cover his pirate flag with the treasure that he had collected. He carefully covered the skull and crossbones with pebbles and then said, 'I need more treasure!' and he climbed back down again. This time he went to the bushes at the bottom of the play area and collected leaves. He carried them back on board his ship and carefully placed them on the pirate flag saying, 'Cover it all up, me hearties!'

Cassie (14 months) climbed into the ball pool and attempted to cover herself up with the balls. She used her hands like paddles moving the balls towards her head and body and laughed.

Jeevan (4 years 2 months) made a den on the sofa in his childminder's house using a throw and some cushions. He climbed underneath it and said, 'I'm being a bear in my secret cave. No one knows where I am because they can't see me.'

The enveloping schema can be identified if children are repeatedly covering or enclosing themselves or other objects. We may see children:

- drawing a picture or painting and then covering it with a wash of paint
- painting the whole paper from edge to edge
- painting their whole hand, palm and back with paint or glue
- dressing up in layers of clothing, cloaks or saris
- wearing lots of hats
- wrapping up toys and objects in paper or cloth
- showing a keen interest in putting things in envelopes
- wrapping presents repeatedly
- hiding, camouflaging or concealing themselves with material and drapes
- covering their face with flannels when bathing
- playing games such as peek-a-boo or hide and seek
- hiding in spaces, boxes, under table cloths, behind curtains or under duvets
- showing a particular interest in dens and tunnels
- burying themselves or objects in sand.

So what? Interpreting the enveloping schema

Laura is really enjoying playing this game with her dad. When he asks, 'Where's Laura gone?', Laura is still working out whether or not her dad can still see her when she hides behind the curtain. She is consolidating her understanding of object permanence, the idea that something exists even when she can't see it. This develops at quite a young age, at around seven or eight months, although it is not fully understood until around two years. The turn taking aspect of their game will also benefit her development of conversation, which relies on a good ability to take it in turns.

Naresh was playing a similar game with his friend Julia, putting the netting over his head and waiting for Julia to remove it. He did this repeatedly and they both enjoyed the hiding aspect of the game. They were exploring the concept of hiding and being unseen. Naresh exclaims, 'I see you', sounding surprised that he could still see through the netting. He is exploring the idea of transparency and relating this to different materials. This 'peek-a-boo' sort of play also helps children to reinforce their understanding of cause and effect and allows them to engage in turn taking, assisting in learning the art of conversation.

Cassie is being very physically active as she plays in the ball pool, moving her arms and hands to manoeuvre the balls towards her body. She is developing her gross motor skills and also exploring the movement of the balls. She appears to be trying to cover herself up with the balls, which could indicate an interest in enveloping, and it could link with a trajectory schema as she enjoys the movement aspects of this play.

Hayden is in role as he collects treasure (stones and leaves) to cover his pirate flag. It is clear that he wants to cover the flag with treasure, and his use of language helps to identify this when he states, 'Cover it all up, me hearties!' This play may also link with a positioning schema as Hayden is very precise about where he places the pebbles – he covers the crossbones meticulously.

Again, it is Jeevan's language that gives us the clue as to what he is doing. He is clearly hiding and investigating being hidden and who can and can't see him. He is also showing an interest in bears and caves and we can tap into this to support and extend his play.

What next? Extending the enveloping schema

We can support and extend children's interest in enveloping in many ways. Laura might enjoy playing hide and seek around the house with her dad or hiding under a table with a cloth over it and making an enclosed space in which to play. She might also like to play a guessing game where she and her dad take it in turns to hide a toy and guess which toy is hidden.

We could extend the play of Naresh and Julia by offering them plenty of different materials to use to cover themselves or with which to build dens. They might enjoy making a den with a clothes horse and sheet, attaching it with clothes pegs or playing together in a play tent. Alternatively, they might want to fill containers and create lids out of material to cover up the contents of the containers.

We can pick up on Cassie's interest in playing in the ball pool and perhaps introduce her to a soft-play centre or larger ball pool. She may also like to explore sand or pebbles at a beach. She can use similar movements with her arms to scoop up pebbles or sand and explore the new sensory experience that this would offer.

Burying some treasure for Hayden to find in the sand tray might interest him in extending his play around pirates and pirate ships and enveloping. He might want to hide some gold coins by wrapping them in large leaves and tying some string around them or create some treasure maps which he can put into envelopes and give to his friends.

Jeevan might enjoy finding out about camouflage and how animals hide from predators. He may also enjoy reading stories about bears, such as *We're Going on a Bear Hunt*[1] or *Can't You Sleep Little Bear?*,[2] and then perhaps creating his own bear cave to hide in.

If we identify an enveloping schema in the children in our care, we will want to support and extend their thinking by providing additional activities or resources. Here are some suggestions for extending the enveloping schema:

- Provide access to tents and den-building materials.
- Offer children large pieces of material or old pillow cases and cushion covers.
- Provide large boxes to climb into.
- Give children access to wrapping paper and wrapping activities.
- Offer mark-making materials and envelopes of different shapes and sizes.
- Visit the local post office, then create a post office in the role play area.
- Provide different types of material for wrapping toys and objects, e.g., fur, satin, fleece, netting.
- Provide posting toys, shape sorters and stacking cups.
- Offer boxes with lids or material to cover baskets and pots.
- Encourage children to paint toys or stones.
- Offer opportunities to fold paper.
- Create wax pictures with a wash of paint covering them or scratch art pictures where the design is created by scratching away a layer.
- Ensure that dressing up and role play areas include hats, scarves and cloaks.

- Provide bandages and cloths for wrapping up parts of the body.

- Provide small clothes or blankets for swaddling the dolls.

- Allow children to bury themselves or objects in a sand pit or at the beach.

- Play pass the parcel.

- Offer children access to hand puppets or make sock puppets for children to put their hands in.

- Play hide and seek or guessing games like 'hedgehogs down' (where we hide children and the children have to guess who is hidden) or 'Kim's game' (where we hide objects from a tray).

- Play parachute games that involve going under the parachute or making it like a tent.

- Offer cooking activities that include wrapping food or spreading, e.g., wraps, tacos, sausage rolls, pasties, pasta parcels, spreading butter on toast or passata on pizza.

- Use language such as full, empty, in, out, underneath, under, over, hide, hidden, disappear, transparent, camouflage, visible, invisible, unwrap, wrap, cover up, envelop.

Links with other schemas

The enveloping schema links closely with enclosing (see Chapter 6) and containing (see Chapter 4) as children are fascinated with enveloping objects and themselves. Laura may also enjoy enclosing herself in boxes, which would demonstrate a link with enclosing. Naresh and Julia might like to fill and empty containers, covering up the contents with lids or pieces of material, which links closely with containing.

Cassie is exploring the movement of the balls in the ball pool, which could be classed as trajectory (see Chapter 12), therefore it is difficult to identify the true motives for her play. We can simply observe more and offer her opportunities to extend her play, noting her responses and adjusting our provision accordingly. Hayden is positioning the stones carefully as he covers the flag, which indicates a link to the positioning schema (see Chapter 10). His language helps us to understand what he is trying to achieve, although we could also offer him additional opportunities to extend his interest in positioning.

References

1. Rosen, M. (1993) *We're Going on a Bear Hunt*. London: Walker Books Ltd.
2. Waddle, M. (2002) *Can't You Sleep Little Bear?* Somerville, MA: Candlewick Press.

Chapter 8

Going Through a Boundary

CHAPTER OBJECTIVE

This chapter will share stories about children who are interested in going through a boundary, for example, having a fascination with doors and windows or moving things into and out of spaces. It will offer ideas of what to observe, how to interpret it and how to extend this play in terms of activities and resources.

What? Observing the going through a boundary schema

We go through boundaries regularly without even noticing them. Every time we pass through a doorway or post a letter, we are going through a boundary. Some children become fascinated with this concept and want to explore the idea of something or themselves going through a boundary and emerging at the other side.

Jack (3 years 8 months) is playing with the door flap of a tent. He opens it and closes it and moves his head in and out of the space again and again. He says, 'Open, close, open, close' and 'In, out, in, out'. He gets cross when his older brother says, 'Shake it all about,' and replies, 'No! In, out, in, out!'

Mollie (2 years 5 months) went to the shopping centre with her mum and wanted to repeatedly go through the automatic doors that operated at the entrance. After the third or fourth time of going through, Mollie's mum moved her on. Later, when they were going through the doors on the way back to the bus stop, Mollie wanted to explore the doors again and go back and forth. She would have continued for much longer if her mum had not whisked her home for tea.

When Georgia (2 years 11 months) went to the playground, she was particularly interested in the tunnel and spent a long time repeatedly crawling through it, running round and crawling through again. She later experimented with direction and went back through the other way.

Naresh (15 months) is exploring the shape sorter. He holds each piece and tries to post it through the holes. After he has successfully inserted a piece into the appropriate hole, the shape sorter lights up and plays a short tune. Naresh puts his hand into the hole that he has just posted a shape through. Then he picks up the shape sorter, brings it closer to his face and looks inside. His key person says, 'Where's it gone, Naresh?' and this pattern is repeated until Naresh has posted all of the shapes.

Nikzad (3 years 7 months) enjoys playing with the wooden train set. He builds a track and then focuses his attention on the bridges and tunnels. Nikzad moves a train with his hand under a bridge, then back again, and moves it back and forth repeatedly. His key person has noticed that he is particularly interested in how trains go through tunnels and has provided some different-sized tubes for him to explore. He also spends time in the outside area going through spaces, often pretending to be his favourite train, 'Thomas', going through a tunnel.

The going through a boundary schema can usually be observed when children are particularly interested in 'causing oneself or material or an object to go through a boundary and emerge at the other side'.[1]

We may see children:

- crawling through tunnels

- moving trains or cars through tunnels and under bridges

- engaging in threading activities

- crashing toy cars into walls

- playing with water or sand, using funnels, water wheels and sieves, watching the water or sand move through the objects or playing with plugs and plugholes

- using string or rope to tie knots

- using marble runs

- being interested in going through doors or other boundaries

- posting objects into holes or pushing materials through holes

- placing rings over posts.

So what? Interpreting the going through a boundary schema

Children who are particularly interested in this schema might be especially fascinated with the movement it involves – under, over, in, out. Jack is exploring this schema. He continually moves his head in and out of the tent flaps and explores how the flaps of the tent door open and close. He is thinking about moving into and out of the space and considering how his world looks from inside and outside. He gets cross when his brother interrupts his play and insists that he is focusing on the in-ness and out-ness of his game rather than merely singing a song. As he explores this concept, he develops his understanding of beginnings and endings, volume and capacity.

Mollie has a fascination with doors that open and close. This could be interpreted as an interest in the automation of the 'magic doors'. However, she did not spend a long time watching the doors open and close; she was particularly drawn to moving herself in and out of the doorway, which indicates that she was more interested in going through a boundary.

Georgia is exploring crawling through tunnels. She is working out how to travel through an enclosed space, what it is like to be inside the space and how it feels to move through and emerge at the other side. What will happen if I change direction? Will it feel the same if I go back the other way? It would be interesting to note whether Georgia also enjoys enclosing herself in spaces.

Naresh was posting the shapes into the shape sorter and appeared to be fascinated with the boundary of the hole. He looked at it carefully and used his hand to go through the hole, possibly exploring where the shapes went or how to make the music play. His interest in looking inside could imply that he was exploring 'in-ness' and could also indicate a link with a containing schema. His key person recognised this by asking him where the shape had gone.

Nikzad was particularly interested in moving his trains through the tunnels and tubes that his key person had provided. He was thinking critically about length and width. Will this train fit in this tube? Is it long enough for the whole train to be enclosed? Will my hand and arm fit in to push it through?

What next? Extending the going through a boundary schema

When children are exploring this schema, it is important to note if they are particularly interested in doors or windows, because of the potential safety issue. Adults need to be vigilant and if they observe an interest that could lead to a child going through doors or windows, they must talk to the child and their parents/carers to discuss ways of supporting this schema while keeping the child safe. Some things are non-negotiable and we need to teach children that we have rules to keep them safe.

We can offer Jack further opportunities to explore inside and outside by proving materials that he can use to build dens. Jack may want to consider the idea of in-ness by filling and emptying containers or look at putting himself or his toys 'in' other spaces.

For Mollie, it was actually passing through the door that she was particularly fascinated with, so we can offer Mollie opportunities to engage in small world play using resources that have doors to open, close and move toys through. She may enjoy exploring the doors of a doll's house for example. If it appears that her interest only relates to moving herself through doors, we can offer her safe opportunities to do this. Within the home there would be many opportunities to look at doorways and we can use this as an opportunity to help her to learn how to keep herself safe. We can talk to Mollie about holding hands when going through the door or offer her choices about which doors she can go through again and again and reinforce that the front door at home is not one of them.

To support and extend Georgia's exploration of tunnels we may want to offer her the opportunity to play in a pop-up tunnel or see whether she would be interested in exploring a marble run or rolling balls through lengths of drainpipe. Naresh may also want to use different resources to investigate this concept further. He might be interested in posting things or putting rings on posts, all of which also 'go through a boundary'. Nikzad's key person has already recognised his schema and is extending it by offering him different-sized tubes to explore and investigate.

If we recognise the going through a boundary schema in any of our children, we will want to provide additional resources or plan activities that further support and extend their thinking. Here are some suggestions for how we can support children who show a fascination with going through a boundary:

- Offer opportunities for children to crawl through tunnels.

- Encourage children to move into and out of spaces and offer access to den-building materials.

- Encourage children to use construction resources to make bridges and spaces that they can move toys through and under.

- Provide cardboard tubes or pieces of drainpipe to enhance our small world play, particularly the train track.

- Allow children to explore 'in' and 'out' in different contexts, and use positional language to support their play.

- Provide opportunities for threading and weaving.

- Plan for children to embark on sewing projects, using a blunt cross-stitch/tapestry needle or a plastic needle. Commercially produced templates are available that already have holes in to make the stitching easier.

Children with this schema will particularly enjoy going in and out with the needle and thread.

- Offer access to wool, ribbon and long pieces of material which can be woven through a fence.

- Provide different opportunities for posting and create 'post boxes' by cutting a slit in the top of a cardboard tube or shoe box.

- Take the children to post letters into a real post box.

- Provide short lengths of rope and thick string for children to tie knots.

- Offer children opportunities to place rings over posts.

- Engage in sand and water play, offering plenty of objects that the sand and water can move through, e.g., water wheel, funnels, bottles, sieves.

- Provide garlic presses and extruders for use with playdough.

- Provide pieces of material for peek-a-boo type games or allow children to hide behind the curtains.

- Provide marble runs or create your own on a larger scale with drainpipes, guttering and tennis balls.

- Allow children to open and close doors, ensuring their safety is paramount.

- Take the children to a shopping centre or similar area where they will encounter different types of doors to go through, including automatic doors.

- Provide doll's houses or small world resources with doors and windows that children can open and close and move objects through.

- Create a fixings board with different sorts of latches, handles, bolts and locks.

- Make a circuit for children to follow which involves tunnels, doorways, arches or gates.

- Create or purchase hanging doorway curtains which children go through, e.g., bead-strings or flower-strings.

- Provide shape sorters and resources that encourage children to post objects into spaces.

- Use words such as in, out, through, in between, tunnel, under, over, on top, below, thread, doorway, window, door, opening, arch, bridge and hole, to support this schema.

Links with other schemas

Children who are interested in going through a boundary often also show an interest in enclosing (see Chapter 6) and enveloping (see Chapter 7). They may want to explore moving into and out of spaces and covering themselves, playing peek-a-boo type games. Jack was engaged in this type of play with the door flap of the tent. We may also notice links with children interested in containing (see Chapter 4), as children post objects into post boxes or shape sorters. Naresh also shows a strong interest in playing with post boxes and putting rings on posts. Children who are fascinated by moving objects or themselves through a boundary might also show an interest in the position of objects (see Chapter 10) or be fascinated by their orientation (see Chapter 9). Georgia was interested in changing direction while moving through the tunnel, which could imply links with an orientation or positioning schema.

References

1. Arnold, C. and The Penn Green Team (2010) *Understanding Schemas and Emotion in Early Childhood*, p.22. London: Sage.

Chapter 9

Orientation

CHAPTER OBJECTIVE

This chapter will share case studies about children who are interested in seeing things from different angles, for example, children looking through their legs, or lying on their backs with their legs up, or lying upside down on a sofa. It will suggest what sort of behaviours to observe, attempt to interpret this behaviour and offer ideas of how to extend this play in terms of activities and resources.

What? Observing the orientation schema

Movement is essential to babies and young children. Initially, babies can only view the world from the place where they are held or are lying. Once babies become more mobile, they are able to roll over, crawl, cruise and eventually stand up to view the world differently. As they grow, they discover that things look different from different angles and positions. It is in discovering this effect of movement that the orientation schema begins.

Johnny (18 months) and his brother Dexter (2 years 6 months) could often be seen upside down. They looked through their legs at the television and Dexter hung upside down from the climbing frame. They both enjoyed seeing the world from different angles.

Sally (4 years 2 months) lifted the large conch shell closer to her eyes, then tilted her head to one side, looked closely at the shell again, and tilted her head to the other side. She carefully turned the shell over in her hands before holding it up above her head and leaning backwards, looking at the underneath of the shell. 'When I look up there, I can see the hole, but when I look down here it's gone.' After a minute or two Sally sat down and held the shell in both hands. She looked down at it and continued to study the shell for several minutes.

Hayden (3 years 5 months) is interested in viewing things through different lenses and will often use magnifying glasses to explore objects and the world around him.

Sammy (3 years 2 months) liked exploring the world from different heights. At the park she always chose to climb up to the top of the climbing frame and would also frequently lie on the ground or on slides. Her key person noticed that she would often stand on the tree stumps in the outdoor area, lie on the rug in the book corner, and had a particular interest in how far away things were from her. Her parents shared that she always asked to have a ride on her father's shoulders and could often be heard chanting, 'I'm the queen of the castle...'

Juliette (5 years 2 months) went through a phase of taking her binoculars everywhere. She was particularly interested in how things looked and how they changed in size, and would prefer visual cues, pictures and photographs. On one occasion, Juliette looked through the binoculars the other way round and noticed that things looked further away. She regularly used words such as look, see, big and bigger.

The orientation schema can often be observed when children are particularly interested in looking at things from different angles. The case studies illustrate this.

We may see children:

- moving themselves and their bodies into different positions
- appearing fascinated by different heights or perspectives
- lying down on the floor and other surfaces
- hanging upside down from climbing frames
- looking through their legs
- rolling, spinning, twisting their bodies
- often choosing to swing during free play
- moving objects to view them from different angles
- building ramps and steps to see things from a higher viewpoint
- climbing up whenever possible
- looking through holes and peeping though gaps
- repeatedly using magnifying glasses, binoculars, kaleidoscopes and telescopes.

We are most likely to see this schema when children are involved in investigation and exploration of objects and during play that involves movement.

So what? Interpreting the orientation schema

Some children may have the urge to hang upside down, to lie with their legs up on the sofa and their heads hanging off it, or to bend down and look through their legs. This behaviour can be perplexing to adults, who may respond by asking the child to sit up again, although for a younger child they may find this endearing or amusing. These children are all exploring their world and trying to make sense of what they see. Does the shell look the same from every angle? Does the whole world go upside down when I am upside down? They explore their ideas and, as they explore them, their theories are either confirmed or challenged.

Johnny and Dexter will find that the whole world is not upside down when we look through our legs. Their thinking is challenged. They are exploring this concept and working out their understanding of what upside down means.

Sally, who is closely examining the shell, will find that it does indeed look different from different angles. She will notice the intricate pattern and the subtle changes in colour and texture on the top compared with the smooth surface underneath the shell. Taking in new information like this is what Piaget[1] called *assimilation*. Sally will then use the new information that she is learning to adjust her previous thinking about the shell, which Piaget termed *accommodation*.

Hayden is particularly interested in how things look through different lenses. He is building a picture of the world from his individual viewpoint and each time he looks through a lens he adds more detail to his understanding. He is constructing knowledge through his exploration of this schema, and Athey[2] would say that he is contributing to his 'forms of thought' and developing concepts. In other words, he is exploring the world and attempting to make sense of it.

Sammy, on the other hand, is particularly interested in exploring her view of the world from different heights. She is beginning to explore concepts relating to height and depth through climbing, space, distance and proximity and through lying in various places and noticing how the world looks from different viewpoints.

Juliette, like Hayden, also likes to look through lenses. Her fascination for viewing situations through her binoculars can also be noted through the language she uses. She describes her understanding of how her view changes when she looks through the binoculars in terms of 'big' and 'bigger'. Taking notice of children's language as well as their actions will help us to further interpret their schematic behaviour.

What next? Extending the orientation schema

We can extend children's fascinations in orientation in many ways. For example, Johnny and Dexter might like to engage in soft play where they can crawl through tunnels, climb over and under bridges or obstacles and use their bodies in different ways. Sally might enjoy using a magnifying glass to explore her shells in more detail, and Hayden might enjoy being offered additional opportunities to look through coloured lenses and binoculars.

We could extend Sammy's exploration of height, adding in the idea of perspective by taking her for a walk up a hill and looking at things far away, for example, sheep in a field, pointing out that they appear to be smaller. This is what Juliette noticed when she looked through the other end of the binoculars and could be extended by asking her questions relating to distance, for example, 'What do you notice when you look through the binoculars?' and 'What happens when you turn them the other way round?'

If we recognise this schema in any of our children, we may like to consider providing additional resources or planning an activity to support and extend their thinking. Here are some suggestions showing how we can support children who show a fascination for seeing things from different angles:

- Play games that involve children moving their bodies into different positions, rolling, rocking and twisting.

- Offer opportunities to climb or hang from climbing frames or trees, bearing in mind safety issues.

- Provide rocking horses or rocking toys they can sit on in the outside area.

- Allow children to explore things such as tables and slides by getting underneath them.

- Provide objects to climb on so children can view things from different heights.

- Provide resources for children to look through: telescopes, magnifying glasses, binoculars, kaleidoscopes, coloured lenses.

- Provide mirrors for children, hand held and fixed to walls or floors so they can see themselves from different angles.

- Make holes in material or wood for children to look through.

- Provide holes to peep through, e.g., a keyhole or letterbox in the playhouse, windows in the doll's house. Or go for a walk and search for holes in the local environment.

- Make pin-hole cameras out of cardboard tubes or peep holes in boxes.

- Make binoculars, telescopes and kaleidoscopes out of rolled-up tubes of paper.

- Engage in soft play as it can allow children opportunities to roll, twist, climb and view the world from different angles.

- Provide 3D glasses or make your own with red and blue clear cellophane sweet wrappers and provide 3D pictures for children to explore.

- Offer mats and soft surfaces on which children can do headstands or lie down.

- Offer access to rope and tyre swings as well as traditional swings as they allow children to explore viewing the world while swinging.

- Teach the children some yoga moves.

- Provide opportunities to play with pendulums or to observe a Newton's cradle.

- Cover some windows or create stained-glass windows to look through with tissue paper or coloured film.

- Create a sensory box with objects hanging inside and peepholes for children to look through and guess what the objects are.

- Use language to support this schema, such as look through, twist, forwards, backwards, spinning, under, over, upside down.

Links with other schemas

It is fairly common for children who are interested in orientation to also show an interest or fascination in positioning (see Chapter 10) and rotation (see Chapter 11) schemas. They may link their investigation into viewing the world from different angles to the position of objects or how they move, for example, Hayden regularly lines things up and can be particular about where things are positioned. Johnny was also particularly interested in spinning himself around, and both he and Dexter loved rolling down hills, implying a possible rotation schema. In addition, Sally would often group things very carefully so that they were touching each other, which could be interpreted as a positioning schema. In Chapter 8 we also saw Georgia, who was interested in changing direction as she moved through a tunnel, which could be interpreted as an interest in orientation as well as going through a boundary.

References

1. Piaget, J. (1951) *Play, Dreams and Imitation in Childhood*. London: Routledge and Paul.
2. Athey, C. (2007) *Extending Thought in Young Children: A Parent–Teacher Partnership* (2nd ed.). London: Sage.

Chapter 10

Positioning

CHAPTER OBJECTIVE

This chapter will share examples of children who are interested in where things are and positioning items in lines, rows or by size. It will offer ideas of how to extend this play in terms of activities and resources.

What? Observing the positioning schema

Have you ever gone for a coffee and been totally distracted by a picture frame that is not hanging horizontally, or found yourself rearranging the dishes after someone else has stacked the dishwasher! The position of objects is very important at times and some children will line up their toys or place items very carefully in specific places – and woe betide anyone who touches them! The positioning schema is about children who place themselves or objects in specific positions and are interested in where things are.

Lydia (2 years 10 months) searched through the box of animals and found all the elephants. She then placed them side by side. Lydia was particularly interested in making a line and spent a long time putting each elephant in place. She seemed to have a clear idea of where she wanted each elephant to go. She told her childminder about her line, saying, 'This is the daddy elephant, this vis the baby elephant, this is the big sister elephant, this is the tiny baby elephant, this is the mummy elephant and this is the auntie elephant!'

Ewan (2 years 10 months) is very particular about food and has recently started attending full days at nursery. One lunchtime he got very upset when he was given spaghetti bolognaise and started to cry, refusing to eat it, even though his mum had told staff that he liked it. Ewan was repeatedly saying, 'Not on top, not on top!' One practitioner then decided to give him some bolognaise in a bowl and he ate it, and afterwards she offered him some spaghetti, which he ate too. The practitioner realised that he didn't want the spaghetti and the bolognaise mixed up together.

During the morning session, Carlos (3 years 4 months) was playing with the cars on the car mat and lining up the cars side by side. His key person asked him if he would like to make a garage for his cars to line up in and he agreed. So they used an old shoe box and she helped him to draw lines inside the box to mark out parking spaces. She then drew a large P in a blue circle on the back wall of the garage. Carlos used the garage immediately, filling each parking space with cars.

Caitlin (15 months) learned to walk at 13 months and has since become very confident at exploring new spaces. She is particularly interested in lying on the floor, crouching under tables and chairs and exploring different positions.

Jane (3 years 5 months) rummaged in the toy box and collected a handful of objects, placing them in a pile on the floor. She then began to lay them all out in a line, beginning with the blue items, then red, then brown. Jane spent a long time creating this line and then told her sister not to touch it. She said it was like a long train.

The positioning schema is often seen when children line up objects or position themselves in some way. We may see children:

- lining up toys in rows or side by side
- ordering objects and toys by size, colour or shape
- sorting toys into mummy, daddy and baby
- placing toys or objects in specific places and being obsessive about where items are placed
- preferring to have food separated on their plate
- always wanting to sit in a certain place
- always wanting to be at the front or back of a line

- frequently putting things on their head
- walking around the rim or edge of a sand pit or play area
- lying on the floor or under the table
- getting their bodies into different positions.

So what? Interpreting the positioning schema

Sometimes adults may worry that certain positioning behaviours might be an indicator of something else, for example, *Autistic Spectrum Disorder (ASD)*; however, this is not necessarily the case. Not wanting foods to touch or displaying behaviours such as lining up toys is common behaviour for young children and should not be a cause for concern on its own. To build up a clearer picture of a child's needs we would want to observe that child in many different contexts. For example, if we observed that a child was having difficulty with language and communication, understanding others and being understood, finding it difficult to relate to their peers or displaying some sensory issues, then we might want to investigate further, sharing what we have observed with a Special Educational Needs Coordinator or other professional.

Lydia was sorting and classifying the elephants by picking them out of the animal box and positioning them. She wasn't playing a game with the elephants as some children do, making them walk or talk to each other, but she was carefully placing each of them in a specific place and giving them a name. She was exploring her understanding of family and developing the mathematical concepts of ordering and sequencing. She was thinking critically and learning organisational skills, such as planning where each elephant was going to be placed. These skills develop into the sorts of skills needed for everyday life as we organise our work schedules and plan our time.

Ewan does not want foods to touch each other. Many children go through this phase, for example, liking sponge and custard but not custard on sponge. Ewan's key person recognised this behaviour and was easily able to offer him his spaghetti in a different bowl from his bolognaise. It would be interesting to note whether Ewan is also particular about other things, for example where he sits. Sometimes children have a strong sense of what is right – the right way to serve a particular food, or the right place to sit – and this is linked to routines and rituals. Young children prefer a constant routine, often choosing to do things the same way over and over again. This gives them a sense of security and safety as they know what will happen and how it will happen. It could be that being offered food that looked 'wrong' to Ewan was upsetting as he wasn't sure what it was and what it would taste like. On its own, Ewan could recognise it as bolognaise or spaghetti, but together it looked like something else which was strange and unfamiliar to him. It is easy to allow children like Ewan to have their foods separated and it avoids any potential anxieties about meal times.

Carlos was showing an interest in lining up cars rather than driving them on the road mat. He was also being very purposeful and methodical about where he placed them. Each car needed its own space and he was paying attention to detail in his play. This links with enclosing (see Chapter 6) and one-to-one correspondence – one car to one parking space –which is a really useful tool when counting objects. When counting, we need to say one number name per object, using one-to-one correspondence, otherwise we are not accurately measuring quantity, but simply reciting numbers in order.

Caitlin was developing her understanding of spatial awareness and her proprioceptive sense, where her body is in space. When we are very young, we are learning about how big our body is, what it can do and how we can do it. This constantly changes as our body grows and develops. Caitlin is exploring these concepts as she experiments with squeezing into different spaces. What shape do I need to make my body into to climb under the chair? Will I fit in? Can I stay crouched down, or will I need to sit down? Caitlin is challenging herself physically with these explorations as she develops her gross motor skills, balance and coordination.

Jane created order out of the chaos of mixed-up toys in the box. She actively searched for meaning as she made links between the different pieces, using colour as her criteria. Jane paid attention to the detail of each piece, maintained focus and concentration, and was engaged and motivated as she initiated this play. She was also very protective of her creation, not wanting her sister to touch it as she explored her sense of ownership.

What next? Extending the positioning schema

Lydia's interest in positioning may mean that she would like the opportunity to organise and position other toys. She might also be interested in ordering toys by size. We could also create a small world scene or home for her to place the elephants in using a builder's tray.

For Ewan we can extend his thinking about foodstuffs touching by allowing him to try foods that are mixed together, perhaps involving him in the cooking or preparation process so that he can see how each food is prepared. He needs opportunities to make links with his understanding of spaghetti. Is it still spaghetti if it is mixed with penne pasta? Is it still spaghetti if it is in a sauce? Is it still spaghetti if it has cheese sprinkled on top? Over time, through investigating his food further, Ewan will come to realise that 'spaghetti is spaghetti is spaghetti', and although he may still choose not to mix foodstuffs, it is hoped he will not feel frightened or anxious as it will be much more familiar to him.

Carlos's key person picked up on his positioning schema and extended his interest by suggesting that they make the garage together. This gave Carlos an additional way to organise his cars, placing one at a time into each parking space. We could build on his interest outside by encouraging him to make parking spaces for the bikes, replicating his indoor play on a larger scale.

We can support and extend Caitlin as she investigates positioning in terms of space and her own body by offering her opportunities to play in enclosed spaces such as boxes and play tents. We can ask her questions which encourage her to think about space, for example, 'Will you fit in there?' Bearing in mind her age and stage of development, our questions will need to be concrete and relate to what she can see and feel around her.

Jane might be interested in grouping and classifying other things by colour. We can challenge her thinking by asking her to talk about her line of objects or explain how she created it. It can be challenging for a child to explain what they have done and why, as this requires higher-level thinking skills, analysis, justification and reasons for actions.

Here are a few ideas of how we could extend the positioning schema if we identify it in any of the children in our care.

- Encourage the children to lay the table and create place settings with spaces drawn for knife, fork, spoon, plate and cup.

- Provide tyres, crates and boxes in different places and at different heights for children to climb on and move.

- Allow children to create their own scene in a shoe box for small world play.

- Ensure that we provide enough materials so that children can group things in different ways.

- Encourage children to sequence familiar stories or cycles, e.g., The Gingerbread Man or The Lifecycle of a Butterfly.

- Make patterns with mosaics, collages, peg boards and bead necklaces.

- Offer access to groups of objects, e.g,. Daddy bear, Mummy bear and Baby bear, or lots of different small world people.

- Offer toys and resources that lend themselves to sorting activities.

- Encourage children to make caterpillars and trains.

- Provide name tags for pegs, trays and desks so that children can sit in the same place.

- Offer children opportunities to create constructions where everything can have a specific place, using materials that join or stick together.

- Provide a selection of toys and resources that children can place in different positions.

- Use language associated with size and positioning: next to, behind, on top, under, in front, edge, beside, first, second, third, big, bigger, biggest, small, smaller, smallest.

Links with other schemas

The positioning schema links closely with the orientation schema (see Chapter 9) – as children explore where things or themselves can be positioned, they often look at things from different angles. Caitlin is interested in moving her body into different spaces and is probably also interested in how the world looks from under the chair. She may also have an interest in enclosing (see Chapter 6) or enveloping (see Chapter 7) as she climbs into small spaces and explores space around her.

The positioning schema can link with containing (see Chapter 4) when children place toys in different containers, if they are classifying, grouping and sorting them in some way. It can also link with connecting (see Chapter 3) if children are specifically interested in the position of objects as they join them together and going through a boundary (see Chapter 8).

Chapter 11

Rotation

CHAPTER OBJECTIVE

This chapter will share stories about children who are interested in circular movements, either objects or spinning and rolling themselves. It will offer ideas of how to extend this play in terms of activities and resources.

What? Observing the rotation schema

Circular movement and circles are all around us in our environment, from wheels and cogs to clocks and rolling pins. We write using predominantly anti-clockwise movements, and the earth spins on its axis while moving in a circular motion around the sun. Sometimes we might observe children who have a particular interest and fascination in circles or rotational movement.

From an early age Hannah showed an interest in the washing machine. As soon as she could sit unaided, she would sit and watch the machine spinning! These photos show Hannah at eight months old and 17 months old choosing to sit and watch the machine. She was fascinated by it and even tried to climb into the machine at times.

Coral (2 years 2 months) was at a family wedding and noticed the glitter ball rotating above her. She looked up at it and began to move her head in time with the rotating ball. Then she noticed that the disco lights were moving in circles on the floor and she began to run in circles, following the lights. Coral then lay spread-eagled on the floor and began to use her legs to move her whole body in circles while looking up at the rotating glitter ball.

During a session at nursery, Jack (3 years 11 months) was making some cookies and became very interested in rolling out the dough. His key person showed him how to flatten the dough with his fingers, then gently roll on the rolling pin forwards and backwards to out roll the dough. Jack wanted to do this repeatedly and enjoyed using the rolling pin. He did not show much interest in cutting out the shapes, stating, 'I want to roll it again!'

Liam (4 years) came into nursery very excitedly talking about how his grandad's car had got stuck in the mud. He said, 'The wheels were spinning round like this...', demonstrating by moving his hand really fast through the air in large circles. At the end of the session Liam's key person asked his mum about it and she shared that they had parked the car in a local car park near some woods; it was basically a small field and the heavy rain had made the field very muddy. Liam's grandad was driving and the wheels started spinning. Apparently, Liam thought this was very exciting and loved watching them spinning. He spent the rest of the weekend playing with his toy trucks and cars and making them get stuck in the mud and wheel-spin too!

After it had been raining, Ethan (4 years 8 months) began to spin his Spiderman umbrella upside-down in the outside area. He went inside and collected a white teddy bear and sat the teddy in the centre of the umbrella. He made the umbrella spin and said, 'Teddy is on the roundabout!' Ethan spent a long time spinning the teddy, noticing that when he put teddy in the centre and the umbrella was spinning, teddy moved nearer the outside of the umbrella. He kept stopping and putting teddy back in the centre and was using words like, 'In the middle' and 'Round and round' as he did so. Several of the other children then began to copy Ethan until we ran out of umbrellas!

After eating a sweet from a party bag, Juliette (5 years 10 months) was fascinated with the lolly stick made of paper. She discovered that it could unroll into a flat piece of paper and spent a long time unrolling the paper and rolling it up again. When her Daddy got home from work, she was eager to show him that the lolly stick wasn't really a stick because it unrolled and rolled up again.

The rotation schema is seen when children are fascinated or very interested in circular movement and rotation. Cath Arnold[1] defines the rotational schemas as 'turning, twisting or rolling oneself or objects around'. You may see children:

- spinning round and round on a roundabout or other spinning ride
- spinning, twirling or rotating themselves or objects
- rolling down hills
- repeatedly running in circles or riding a bike in circles
- showing an interest in wheels and wheeled toys
- watching things that rotate, such as the washing machine
- making circular marks in their drawings and paintings
- being fascinated by large wheels on trucks

- turning and twisting knobs on cupboards or toys
- unscrewing jars and bottles
- spinning a globe around and around
- being fascinated by windmills and watching them rotate for a long time
- watching the water going down the plughole
- unrolling the toilet paper
- twisting up the swing and unwinding it again when they are sitting on it.

So what? Interpreting the rotation schema

Hannah's interest in the washing machine could stem from the fact that she frequently watched her mummy loading and unloading it, or possibly because it made a loud noise, but it could also be the fact that the machine rotates and she liked to watch it spinning. Washing machines also vibrate when they spin, making watching it a multi-sensory experience for a young child. It would be interesting to note whether she also expressed an interest in or fascination with things that rotate in other contexts.

Coral had noticed the rotating disco ball and the way that the lights were hitting it and reflecting circular movements on the floor. She was using her gross motor skills in moving her head and running in circles following the lights. This was also a very multi-sensory experience for Coral as she listened to the music, watched the lights and moved her body around. She was developing her *vestibular system* (a system that helps balance and spatial orientation) and learning to balance as she moved her head around. She was also developing her *proprioceptive sense*, which is all about working out where the body is in relation to the space around.

Jack's insistence on rolling the dough again and again indicates an interest in rotation. He enjoyed using his hands to move the rolling pin and was watching the dough flatten as the rolling pin rolled it out. This was also a core and radial movement as his hands moved in a straight line as the rolling pin rotated and the ball of dough flattened. Jack was using hand–eye coordination and developing his manipulative skills.

Liam really enjoyed watching the wheels spin on his grandad's car. He articulately shared with nursery staff how the wheels were 'spinning round like this' and he demonstrated his concept of them spinning using his hand movement. Liam then replicated the wheel-spinning in his play, confirming his fascination with the wheels turning round. Again, this sort of play helps to develop his fine and gross motor skills. Liam was also finding out about what happens to wheels when they are on different surfaces and was beginning to understand about mechanical systems and forces.

Ethan was conducting his own scientific investigation when spinning his umbrella upside-down. When he added his teddy he was also investigating centrifugal force, noticing that when he put teddy near the centre of the umbrella, and spun it, teddy moved out towards the edge. The spinning of the umbrella also necessitated a twisting action with Ethan's hands, which is quite a tricky movement for a four-year-old to master, so Ethan had introduced a high level of challenge into his play.

Juliette noticed that the paper lolly stick was actually made up of a strip of paper that had been rolled up. She was thinking about this carefully and using her powers of observation to look closely at the paper as it unwound, in order to deduce how it was made. She was interested, excited and motivated to investigate this and wanted to share her findings with her dad. She had to have excellent hand–eye coordination for this task as the lolly stick was quite small and fiddly.

What next? Extending the rotation schema

Many of these children are problem solving and investigating why things happen and how the world works. We can support and extend their thinking by engaging in *sustained shared thinking* with them and asking challenging questions or commenting on what we see. We can also think about providing additional contexts or resources that will extend their thinking about rotation. For example, Hannah might enjoy having the opportunity to watch other things that spin, like playing with a spinning top or even using a salad spinner.

We can extend Coral's interest in rotation by offering her opportunities to move her body in circular or rolling movements. She might enjoy rolling down a hill or spinning herself around. Coral may also want to look closely at things that rotate or spin. Can we borrow a disco ball for her to play with? Perhaps we can recreate a disco in the role play area or in a sensory room by making a dark space, including some coloured lights and offer the children torches to play with to shine onto the rotating disco ball. When playing with torches and lights we can also remind children not to shine them into each other's eyes.

Jack might want more opportunities to use rolling pins in other contexts. Can we make sure that the rolling pins are available with playdough? Can we put a rolling pin in a drawer in the home corner? There are some commercially available rolling pins that are textured and leave a mark on the dough when they roll. Jack might find this a fascinating resource to play with. Perhaps we can plan an activity when we use paint rollers to paint with so that Jack can continue his interest in how things roll.

Liam might simply enjoy having a selection of wheels or wheeled toys to explore and investigate. We could pose a few questions such as, 'Do big wheels turn more slowly than small wheels?' or 'Why do you think the wheel was spinning on the car but the car wasn't moving?' and 'How can we help the car to move again?' Through play we can explore and investigate difficult concepts and think deeply about what we find. We can research problems together and model how to find out if we don't know the answer. We can cooperate and work together as a team.

Ethan might like to explore how it feels to go on a roundabout or ride that spins. We could discuss with him what he noticed when he put teddy in the centre of the umbrella. We could ask, 'I wonder why teddy kept moving? Shall we try putting other toys on the umbrella and see what happens?' Perhaps we can continue our experiment at the park on the big roundabout. Will toys stay on the roundabout when it is spinning? What does this remind us to do when we are on the roundabout – hold on!

We could extend Juliette's thinking about the lolly stick, by investigating other things, for example, cardboard tubes, and looking at how they are made. Could we try to make our own stick from rolled-up paper? Can we work out how to make a tube? How are they different? Juliette might also share an interest in rolling and unrolling other things on a larger scale, for example, the car mat or a rug. Can everything be rolled up? What sorts of things do not roll up and what sorts of things do?

If we recognise that children in our care have an interest in rotation and circular movement, we can provide additional resources to extend their thinking. Here are a few suggestions about how to extend the rotation schema:

- Allow children to roll their bodies and practise different ways of moving their bodies in a circular motion.

- Offer opportunities for children to engage in *heuristic play* (i.e., using 'real' objects in an open-ended way) with things that could roll, e.g., round coasters, pencils, tubes, balls, cylindrical bottles, rolling pins.

- Provide resources that are circular, round or spherical, including different sorts of wheels, balls.

- Offer opportunities to play with wind-up toys, spinning tops and toys that spin.

- Take children to a playground with equipment that spins or can rotate, e.g., swings, roundabouts, spinning seats.

- Engage in write–dance activities when children make anticlockwise pre-writing movements along with music.

- Encourage children to investigate kaleidoscopes.

- Offer access to a variety of balls of different sizes and types, e.g., soft, squishy, hard, small, big, and balls that jingle or light up.

- Play circle games with the children, including games that involve moving in circles and parachute games.

- Roll paint-coated marbles in a paper-filled tray to make patterns.

- Use paint rollers or textured rolling pins in paint and long strips of paper to roll onto.

- Make a vortex out of two old cola bottles by gluing them together like a sand time and drilling a hole in each lid to let water through.[2]

- Offer children the opportunity to play with gears and cogs.

- Provide access to a variety of wheeled toys and vehicles.

- Sing songs such as 'The Wheels on the Bus', 'Wind the Bobbin Up', 'Round and Round the Garden' or 'Roly-Poly Roly-Poly'.

- Offer children opportunities to investigate rolling pins and whisks using playdough or during cooking activities.

- Provide bottles and jars with lids that screw and unscrew.

- Give children a salad spinner to play with.

- Demonstrate a spirograph or spinning pictures.

- Provide hoops and tyres to roll around in the outside area.

- Offer children ribbons on sticks to wave in circular patterns.

- Provide opportunities to play with water wheels in sand and water tray.

- Create pin-wheels or use windmills with the children.

- Use language associated with rotation: round, spin, roll, circle, sphere, dizzy, turn, twist, screw, un-screw, rotate, wind-up, unwind, twirl, etc.

Links with other schemas

The rotation schema links most closely with the core and radial schema (see Chapter 5), which combines both rotational and trajectory movement. Jack, Ethan and Juliette potentially share this interest and may be fascinated by the core and radial schema too. Jack enjoys the rolling of the rolling pin and the flattening of the dough; Ethan was investigating centrifugal forces which move an object in a straight line from a central point when moving in a circular motion; Juliette was fascinated by the flat paper rolling into a rounded stick shape. The rotation schema also links with orientation, and children may be interested in spinning or rolling themselves like Dexter and Johnny in Chapter 9.

References

1. Arnold, C. and the Penn Green Team (2010) *Understanding Schemas and Emotion in Early Childhood*, p.22. London: Sage.
2. Incredible Science (2013) *Cyclone Tube Tornado in a Bottle ~ Incredible Science*. Retrieved from https://www.youtube.com/watch?v=oLfZFGcGc_l, accessed 22 May 2017.

Chapter 12

Trajectory

CHAPTER OBJECTIVE

This chapter will share case studies about children whose repeated behaviours include dropping items or food from cots and high chairs, playing with running water from the tap, building and knocking down towers, climbing and jumping off furniture, throwing, bouncing or kicking balls. It will offer ideas of how to extend this play in terms of activities and resources.

What? Observing the trajectory schema

The term trajectory comes from the Latin word *trajectoria*, which literally translated means 'throw across'. So the term trajectory is used to talk about the movement of an object in space or the movement of a person. We talk about the trajectory of an aeroplane, meaning the path that it is taking across the sky. When we think about schemas, we use the term trajectory to talk about the movement or path that objects are taking, for example, dropping or throwing items, the movement of running water or the movement of one's arm or leg when throwing or kicking.

Jack (2 years 10 months) was at the park with his family and playing football with his brother. He was kicking the ball and running after it for a long time. His older brother asked him to try to pass the ball but Jack insisted he should kick the ball saying, 'I kick it!'

Joshua (14 months) woke up from his lunchtime nap and called to his sister Darcy (3 years 7 months), saying, 'Dar, Dar, Dar, Dar'. Darcy rushed to his room and found that Joshua was throwing all of his toys out of his cot and laughing. Darcy threw them back in and Joshua immediately threw them out again. They continued this game for several minutes, laughing together. Their mother entered the room and Darcy said, 'Joshy is throwing his toys, Mummy'. Their mummy picked up the toys and put them back into the cot saying, 'These are your toys, they stay in your cot,' and Joshua threw them out again. Joshua's mummy picked up the toys, firmly said, 'No, Joshua,' and lifted him out of the cot.

While on a nursery outing to a farm park, Deon (4 years 2 months) spends a long time in the play area. He repeatedly slides down the drop slide and does not appear to be interested in any other activities at the farm park. When we asked Deon what he liked, he said, 'The slide because it made me fly!'

In the summer, when her dad used the sprinkler to water the garden, Sammy (4 years 8 months) spent a long time watching the water moving up and down. She began to play with the water and asked if she could get her goggles and get really wet. She spent a long time moving her hands through the water and eventually moving herself through the wall of water.

Georgia (2 years 8 months) always chooses to swing on the swings. She rarely goes on any other equipment when at the park and demands that she is pushed on the swings again and again.

The trajectory schema involves a fascination with how objects and people move and how children can influence these movements. You may see children:

- dropping food or items from a high chair or cot
- jumping and climbing onto and off things, e.g., furniture
- swinging forwards and backwards
- sliding themselves or objects down slides or slopes repeatedly
- throwing objects, toys or balls
- kicking balls or other things
- playing with running water
- pulling tissues out of a tissue box
- rolling a ball down a slope
- running back and forth continuously
- playing with sticks, e.g., moving swords through the air
- building towers and knocking them down.

So what? Interpreting the trajectory schema

Jack demonstrated his interest in kicking the ball rather than playing a game of football, much to his brother's frustration! Jack was insisting through his language that he kick the ball and did not appear interested in passing it to his brother. He is developing his foot–eye coordination and gross motor skills throughout this physical activity. He is also developing his sense of *kinaesthesia* movement (awareness of body). Over time, through repeated experiences of swinging his leg to kick the ball, Jack will learn which movements lead to success and which do not. He will repeat the movements necessary to kick the ball successfully.

Joshua would happily have continued this turn taking, throwing the toys game for longer with his sister; however, it appears that his mum felt exasperated and thus ended the game. This is another example of when schematic behaviour could be construed as bad behaviour (see Chapter 15). Joshua is not being deliberately naughty; he is exploring cause and effect when he drops and throws his toys and they fall to the floor. He is investigating whether or not this happens consistently. He is also enjoying the attention that this activity demands from his sister. These experiments are the beginnings of our understanding of difficult concepts such as gravity and forces, albeit at a very early stage. Games such as this also encourage turn taking, which is an important developmental skill essential for social interaction and conversation. There is plenty of non-verbal communication between Joshua and Darcy in this example. They have had a shared experience and both enjoyed the exchange.

Deon is investigating his own trajectory movement as he slides down the drop slide. This slide is a free-fall slide designed to enable the user to feel weightless for a very brief moment. It sparks the brain's fight or flight response, when our thinking part of the brain is bypassed and we act in terms of emotion and action without rationalising. Dan Goleman[1] calls this 'the amygdala hijacking' as the *amygdala*, part of the brain structures known as our *limbic system*, briefly takes control while we experience some sort of threat, fear or danger. In this state we have increased adrenalin so that we would be able to run our fastest or fight at our strongest if we needed to. The drop slide taps into the desire that many people have to frighten themselves and get an adrenalin rush. Deon is experiencing this and exploring his own ability to move through the air as he drops and slides down the slide. He says that the slide 'made me fly' which articulates his brief feeling of weightlessness and the rush of air past his body as he slides down. Deon is also managing risk for himself. Experiencing risky play will contribute to his natural ability to risk assess for himself, and thus keep him safer in the long run.

Sammy is particularly interested in the movement of the water as it spurts up and cascades down from the sprinkler. Sammy moves her hands through the water. She could be investigating what happens to the flow of water when she moves her hands through, or thinking about the wetness of the water as it touches her hands and arms. Sammy is investigating how water moves and how she can interact with it. Eventually, she moves her whole body through the lines of water and explores the movement of herself and the water in tandem. She asks if she can wear goggles, which not only prevent the water from going in her eyes but also enable her to see as she moves her body through the water. Perhaps she wants to watch what happens to the water as she moves her body through the cascade.

Swinging is a very repetitive movement and is included within the trajectory schema. Through exploring this type of movement; Georgia is moving her body forwards and backwards through the air. She will feel the movement in several ways; through the air rushing past her, through her *proprioceptive sense*, which is the feeling of where her body is in space, and through her vision, as she watches the world swing by. Eventually she will be investigating how to swing the swing by herself and how the movement of her torso and legs can speed up or slow down the swing. Thus, swinging will also contribute to her physical development as she gains an awareness of moving her own body.

What next? Extending the trajectory schema

We can extend the trajectory schema in many ways. For example, Jack may want to investigate kicking different sorts of balls and play other games that involve his foot–eye coordination, for example, hopscotch or stepping stones. We could also tap into his interest in football and introduce a level of skill for him, so that he has to aim the ball into a goal, towards a target, or dribble the ball, passing it from one foot to another.

We could offer Joshua opportunities to throw bean bags or soft toys into containers, or offer him a chance to play a throwing skittles game. He may also be interested in other activities that involve cause and effect, such as some mechanical or technological toys which move or respond when you touch a button, for example, a pop-up electronic toy. Parents and carers could misinterpret Joshua's behaviour as naughtiness (see Chapter 15); however, with an understanding of schemas we can accept the behaviour and plan additional opportunities to extend his thinking.

We may want to take Deon to a theme park where he can explore the feeling of weightlessness further on different rides. Alternatively, we could provide some risky play opportunities for Deon which also involve movement, such as climbing and balancing on play equipment, or den building.

Sammy may relish more opportunities to explore water play in various contexts. She might want to investigate running water from taps, or using washing-up liquid bottles and other containers to pour and squirt water. We could take Sammy to visit some water features in the local environment, such as water fountains, or water play environments in local play parks. Many now cater for water play, providing children with a pump and channels which water flows through. Always bear in mind the dangers that water play can pose and ensure that you risk assess each activity so that children's safety is paramount.

Georgia may want to explore more opportunities to swing herself in different types of swings, for example, rope swings, tyre swings, basket swings. She may also be interested in swinging from other perspectives, such as pendulums and balls tied onto string. We could encourage her to investigate how to move herself on the swing, or see if she wants to push a toy on the swing. This is a challenging activity as usually a child pushes the swing and as the swing moves away from them, they step forwards towards the swing, which, of course predictably swings back towards the child again! Thus, we would want to supervise Georgia's attempts at pushing the swing carefully to ensure that it does not bump into her on its return.

If we recognise the trajectory schema in our children's play, we can support and extend their thinking in many ways. Here are a few suggestions of how we can further develop their thinking about trajectory movements:

- Provide opportunities for children to play with water in a variety of contexts; e.g., different containers and bottles, water wheels, spray bottles, water balloons, playing with running water from pumps, funnels, taps or hosepipes.

- Provide a selection of water pistols and super-soaker guns for them to squirt towards targets on the wall.

- Take children to visit a local adventure playground, park or fountain.

- Offer opportunities for children to move in different ways, e.g., run, jump, climb, swing, slide.

- Investigate pulling and pushing, using yo-yos and pulleys.

- Pretend to move like different animals, e.g., jump like a frog, crawl like a caterpillar, waddle like a duck, swing through the trees like a monkey.

- Encourage risky play such as *forest school*-type activities.

- Provide woodwork tools which use trajectory movements and real opportunities for children to use them, e.g., offer children golf tees to hammer into melons or pumpkins.

- Experiment with dropping objects of different sizes, weights or shapes from different heights.

- Play parachute games with a large parachute or play with toy parachutes.

- Offer the children opportunities to kick balls into goals and around cones, or throw, roll or kick balls to knock down skittles.

- Splatter or flick paint at a large piece of paper or blow paint through straws.

- Investigate pendulum movements, or play swing ball.

- Play a variety of throwing games such as catch, throwing into hoops or buckets or throwing at targets, with a selection of different things, e.g., balls, bean bags, chiffon scarves.

- Make paper planes with children and then throw them to make them fly.

- Investigate catapults and slingshots (if you're brave!).

- Offer access to guttering, tubes and pieces of drainpipe for children to roll balls down or for water to flow along, and provide a variety of materials for children to play with ramps and cars.

- Visit a shopping centre or other building with a glass lift to allow the children to watch the movement up and down.

- Engage in superhero play involving rough and tumble play, playing with swords or pretending to 'fly'.

- Create flags, bunting and kites to use in your outdoor area.

- Engage in bubble play, blowing bubbles, chasing bubbles and trying to catch them.

- Include language such as over, under, on, up, down, fast slow, throw, kick, move, fly, spin, twirl, glide, drop, bounce.

Links with other schemas

The trajectory schema links closely with the core and radial schema (see Chapter 5) as children are interested in the straight lines and rotational aspects of their play. In Chapter 7 we met Cassie who was covering herself with balls in a ball pool. This type of play could be classed as trajectory as well as enveloping as she moves the balls to hide herself.

This schema could also link with containing (see Chapter 4) as children may be interested in the movement of taking things out of containers. For example, some children like to pull all of the tissues out of the tissue box (see Katie in Chapter 15). This could indicate an interest in containing in terms of filling and emptying, but could equally indicate an interest in the physical movement of pulling the tissues outwards and upwards, which could be interpreted as trajectory. In addition, if children are involved in peek-a-boo type games, they will also be moving material, curtains or tent flaps, which links trajectory and containing movements further. However, it does not matter which schema these behaviours fit into; it is more important to consider how this information is used to further support the child.

References

1. Goleman, D. (2006) *Emotional Intelligence: Why It Can Matter More Than IQ.* New York: Bantam Books.

Chapter 13

Transforming

CHAPTER OBJECTIVE

This chapter will share examples of children who like to explore and see changes, for example, adding colour to cornflour, mixing paints together, making or manipulating playdough, adding juice to food to see what happens, adding water to sand and/or making sand moulds. It will offer ideas of how to extend this play in terms of activities and resources.

What? Observing the transforming schema

Many children like to get messy and generally experiment and investigate how materials and substances mix together. When children are particularly interested in how they can influence and change these things, they may be investigating how things transform.

During a free-play session Katie (4 years 10 months) spent a long time investigating the shaving foam. She added some green food colouring and glitter and stirred the mixture using a spoon. She said, 'It's mixing up.'

Twins Harry and Anna (5 years 2 months) love to help their childminder make cakes. They particularly enjoy mixing the ingredients together. When asked why they like baking, Harry answers, 'It's magic, because all the bits change into something else!' Anna adds, 'Like when we have a hard-boiled egg, it changes from runny to hard.'

Lilly-Ann (3 years 9 months) was playing in the mud kitchen outside. She began the session with a bowl of water. She collected some petals and put them in the water, then put a handful of soil into the bowl too. She put her hand in to stir the mud. She appeared to be interested in the way the water turned brown. She added more mud by sprinkling it into the bowl. She continued this play for a long time.

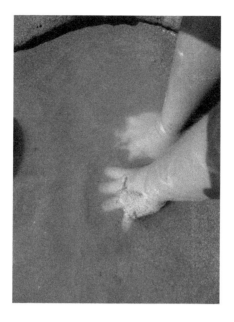

While on holiday with his family, Carlos (3 years 2 months) was digging at the beach with a spade fairly near to the water's edge when he struck water. He put his spade down and began moving his hands in the puddle that he had created, mixing the sand and water together. He then spent a very long time engrossed in this activity. He told his dad, 'The side of my puddle is falling down!'

The transforming schema can be observed when children become fascinated by changing things and mixing things together. It involves investigation, experimenting and looking at cause and effect. You may see children:

- mixing paint to make new colours

- creating mud pies

- adding juice to their mashed potato

- adding different elements to gloop (cornflour and water), e.g., food colouring, glitter

- mixing sand and water together

- enjoying mixing ingredients when cooking

- being fascinated by how some foods change when heated or cooked

- showing an interest in how ice melts and freezes.

So what? Interpreting the transforming schema

Katie is enjoying mixing the food colouring in with the shaving foam. She also adds glitter to her mixture and stirs it with a spoon. Her actions and language confirm her interest in transforming as she talks about mixing it up. Katie is discovering how mixtures can change over time when other elements are added to them. She is mixing colour, adding green to the white shaving foam and making a very light green colour.

Harry and Anna have noticed the transforming nature of cooking. They are fascinated by how the various ingredients change when they are mixed together and heated in some way. Again, this is science in practice and Harry and Anna are using their experience to make links between different cooking activities that they have participated in, both baking cakes and boiling eggs.

Through making her concoction, Lilly-Ann is exploring how things change and this is another example of a transforming schema in action. She is particularly interested in the water changing colour as it gets more and more muddy. Lilly-Ann is experimenting and finding out how different materials change and transform and how she can influence this. If we imagine how a chef might experiment and create a new dish, this is how this sort of play can develop over time.

Carlos is investigating how the sea water changes the sandy puddle. He appears to be particularly interested in how the edges of his hole fall into the water as they become saturated, as he tells his dad about the sides of his puddle falling down. He chooses to use his hands to explore the sandy puddle instead of his spade as this literally allows a hands-on experience. It becomes a multi-sensory experience as he uses his hands to mix the sand and sea water.

What next? Extending the transforming schema

We can extend the transforming schema by tapping into the particular aspect of the experience that the child appears to be fascinated by. For example, Katie might want to explore more colour mixing or messy activities. She could be encouraged to use her knowledge of changing colours to create a colour wheel or 'invent' new colours.

Harry and Anna are particularly interested in how cooking changes the properties of certain ingredients. They might want to go deeper into this thinking and consider how some changes are reversible and other changes are non-reversible. We can begin to use the scientific language associated with this, for example, solid, liquid, dissolve, and solution. The twins might also want to get involved with other cooking activities and make predictions about what might happen and how the ingredients might change.

We can extend Lilly-Ann's thinking by offering her additional opportunities to mix things together – either in the mud kitchen, or through painting, mixing colours or through cooking activities. Carlos may also be interested in these activities, and in addition we could build on his recent experience on holiday by encouraging him to explore sand and water further, perhaps building castles and finding out which consistency of sand makes them the strongest.

We can support and extend the transforming schema in many ways. Here are some suggestions for children who show an interest in how materials transform and change:

- Provide a variety of malleable materials.

- Allow children to investigate ice and how water melts and freezes.

- Freeze some small toy dinosaurs or superhero toys in an ice block and allow children to chip the ice away or investigate how to melt the ice.

- Freeze water-based paints in ice-lolly containers and create your own ice paints.

- Offer plenty of opportunities for cooking.

- Provide a variety of different messy play activities, e.g., jelly, gloop, soap flakes, moon dust, shaving foam, bubble mix.

- Make your own playdough and add sensory ingredients, e.g., rosemary, peppermint flavour, vanilla essence, coffee or chocolate powder, glitter. (Supervise this activity to ensure that children are not tempted to eat it!)

- Experiment with marbling inks.

- Grow things with your children to see how living things change over time.

- Explore decay through collecting leaves and composting vegetable and plants.

- Make rain-makers with oil and water.

- Offer children opportunities to colour mix with paint, chalk, playdough; or place a small amount of two food colouring liquids in small pots and connect them with a piece of kitchen paper – the colours will seep up the paper and mix when they meet.

- Create a mud kitchen or sensory kitchen in your outdoor area.

- Allow children to mix sand and water – if not everyone wants to do this, children can be provided with individual trays.

- Investigate adding water to clay.

- Use language associated with transformation, e.g., change, decay, different, same, time, cook, bake, runny, hard, soft, alter, turn.

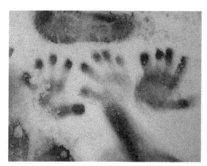 

Links with other schemas

The transforming schema does not appear to link closely to other schemas; however, links may be observed. You could also tap into what you know about individual children, and the schemas that have been identified, to plan specific activities that will capture their imagination. For example, Katie has a clear interest in containing (see Chapter 4) and enclosing (see Chapter 6) and we have now identified a possible interest in transforming. We might want to offer Katie access to paints to colour mix in various bottles and containers and see what happens. She would have the opportunity to mix up various concoctions and fill the containers, which would probably capture her interest.

Chapter 14

Transporting

CHAPTER OBJECTIVE

This chapter will share stories about children moving objects or themselves from one area to another. It will offer ideas of how to extend this play in terms of activities and resources.

What? Observing the transporting schema

Much of our adult life is spent transporting things from A to B: the washing from the machine to the washing line, the shopping from the shops to home, papers and files from desk to briefcase. Many people have a handbag or backpack that they carry things around in and we always carry our clothes or things we might need in rucksacks or suitcases when out for a day's hike or off on holiday. So it should be no surprise that many children imitate this behaviour and can show a keen interest and fascination for moving things around and transporting objects, themselves or others from here to there.

Cassie (1 year 11 months) would often be seen pushing her doll's pushchair around and would fill it will all sorts of toys. It came as no surprise to her mum when her friend Rose visited that Cassie decided to push her around in the pushchair!

Katie (3 years 10 months) walks across the nursery pushing the doll's pushchair. She has loaded it up with several bags which she spent time filling with various bits and pieces. She moves to the small world area and fills up the pushchair seat with people and cars.

Carlos (3 years 4 months) is particularly interested in toys with wheels. While in the outside area, Carlos repeatedly plays with the large dumper truck, filling it with gravel and dirt and then wheeling it to the other side of the play space, before emptying it and wheeling it back. Carlos called out, 'Just one more time!' when he was collecting more gravel and dirt. Later on, Carlos moved all of the gravel and dirt back again in the same way, using the dumper truck to transport the material.

Mary (2 years 10 months) was obsessed with the wheelbarrow at her childminder's house. One day when it had snowed, Mary put her doll in the wheelbarrow and used it like a pram, taking her doll for a walk around the garden. On another occasion, Mary filled the wheelbarrow with other toys and moved them from the play house to the patio and back again.

You may see children:

- pushing toys or other children around in toy pushchairs and buggies

- moving sand or soil in a wheelbarrow from one part of the outside area to another

- filling trolleys with toys and moving them around

- being intent on moving toys and resources to different areas of the nursery or play space

- pushing other children around on bikes, in carts, toy cars, etc.

- carrying a selection of bags and rucksacks

- carrying lots of items in their hands at the same time

- being fascinated with transport, moving things around in wheeled toys

- carrying around a special toy constantly or carrying items to special people.

So what? Interpreting the transporting schema

Cassie has a transporting schema – she loves to move things around from one place to another. She is exploring movement and how to move all sorts of things. By pushing Rose around in the pushchair, she is further extending her ideas of what you can transport. Will Rose fit in the pushchair? Will I be able to push her? Can I move Rose from here to there all on my own?

In Chapter 4 we noted that Katie had a keen interest in containing and it is clear that she also has a transporting schema. Once she has filled bags and containers, she then likes to hang them on the pushchair and move them around the nursery. She also uses the seat of the pushchair as storage, rather than just sitting a doll in it. Katie is thinking about volume and capacity as she loads the pushchair with toys. She is also exploring distance and journeys and how we move things around, for example, will the pushchair fit through this gap in the furniture? Which direction do I need to move in to get to my destination?

Carlos is also thinking about distance as he transports the gravel and dirt from one part of the outside area to another. He is thinking about volume and is both calculating and predicting as he estimates he needs to do one more journey. He is problem solving in a real context and enjoying achieving his goal of moving the dirt and gravel from one area to another. The practitioners are supporting him by providing the large truck and allowing him to move the materials around.

Mary has shown a keen interest in the wheelbarrow. She wants to use it in different contexts and put different toys into it. Mary is not only investigating what will fit in the wheelbarrow but also using her imagination as it becomes a pram for her doll. She is creatively using a toy which has one purpose for another, which demonstrates her creativity and flexible thinking skills.

What next? Extending the transporting schema

We can build on Cassie's fascination with transporting things by offering her alternative ways to do it. She could be interested in filling bags and using them to transport toys from place to place. Cassie might like to have a go on a ride-on bike which has space for her to take a friend on the back. Alternatively, Cassie may want to fill the pushchair with her toys and push it around, perhaps when outside her home.

Tapping into Katie's interest in both containing and transporting, we could offer Katie the opportunity to fill a wheeled suitcase and then go on a journey with it. She might enjoy both packing and travelling to her destination.

We may want to extend her thinking about journeys by creating a map or trail for her to follow or take her on a journey to a travel agency, or even go on a holiday.

We can build on Carlos's interests in transport and transporting things around by offering him an opportunity to investigate the volume and capacity of other trucks and vehicles. We could set up a competition where we count how many journeys it takes with each vehicle to move some sand from A to B and try to work out which truck holds the most sand. Carlos might enjoy visiting a transport museum or watching some real dumper trucks in action.

Mary would benefit from having the opportunity to engage with open-ended materials so that she can be creative and use her imagination. For example, a large construction set with wheels and planks, or a trolley and pieces of material or card, which she can transform into anything she fancies. If we tap into her interest in playing with dolls, we could also offer her opportunities to create something for a doll, for example, a carriage or carry cot.

If you observe children with a transporting schema you will want to extend their thinking further. Here are some ideas to support you:

- Provide buckets, pulley and thin rope for children to explore (ensure activity is supervised).

- Put dumper trucks in your digging area or in a tray with soil, sand or gravel.

- Allow children to transport things using pushchairs, prams, carry-cots, wagons and trolleys.

- Provide trolleys or wheeled toys that are large enough for children to ride on.

- Offer children bikes that have space for a friend or a basket for toys.

- Provide a variety of baskets, bags, purses and rucksacks for children to fill and carry around.

- Allow children to move things from one place to another.

- Supply wheelie bags or suitcases with wheels.

- Provide wheelbarrows in your outdoor area and buckets with handles in your sand area.

- Offer children the opportunity to help carry food to the table, or push the trolley at the supermarket.

- Provide a selection of toys that pull on a string.

- Play with suitcases, packing, unpacking and carrying or wheeling them around.

- Build a small world construction site for moving materials.

- Play 'Pooh-sticks' and make 'boats' out of large leaves to float down a river or stream, ensuring that you fully supervise this activity.

- Encourage children to help to carry clothes from their bedrooms to the washing machine.

- Role play moving house with packing boxes and a toy truck or wagon to fill.

- Go on a scavenger hunt around the garden and collect things in paper bags with handles.

- Encourage play where water can travel along guttering or pipes.

- Use stories and rhymes involving transport or moving things, e.g., *Whatever Next!*[1] or sing 'The Wheels on the Bus'.

- Create a bus or a train with a large box or chairs in a row and imagine going on a journey together.

- Use language to support this schema, such as in, on, full, empty, carry, push, pull, under, on top, right, left, far, near.

Links with other schemas

A clear link between transporting and containing can be identified in children like Katie, who loves to fill bags and containers and move them around. The transporting schema could also link with trajectory (see Chapter 12) if children are interested in the movement aspect of transporting things from one area to another, as trajectory is thinking about the movement of an object or person in space. In a similar way, the transporting schema could also link with a rotation schema (see Chapter 11) if children become fascinated by the wheels and how they move while they transport items from A to B. Carlos might also be interested in both rotation and transporting and we might want to pay close attention to him to see if this is the case.

References

1. Murphy, J. (2007) *Whatever Next!* London: Macmillan.

---- Chapter 15 ----

Reinterpreting Behaviour

CHAPTER OBJECTIVE

This chapter will explore situations where children being engaged in schemas could be misinterpreted as bad behaviour. It will share case studies of different scenarios and offer practical advice for parents and practitioners on how to redirect children's fascinations into more appropriate activities.

What? Observing schematic behaviour

There are many strategies that we use to communicate our needs and wants to other people, and one major way is through how we behave. Behaviour is all about the way in which we conduct ourselves or respond in different situations. Put simply, behaviour is how we act. Children can behave in a manner which could be interpreted as mischievous, misbehaving or deliberate wrongdoing. When an adult does not have an understanding of schematic behaviour, they could 'miss important signals that suggest children's interests and levels of involvement'[1] or simply attempt to dissuade the child from following their pattern of interest.

The National Day Nurseries Association (NDNA)[2] has created a schemas app, a tool devised to assist parents and practitioners in identifying and understanding schemas. Within their introductory blurb to this app, the NDNA states, 'Schemas are often mistaken as negative behaviour when in fact the child is teaching him or herself about the world and how it works.' It is due to this common misdiagnosis that Athey[3] suggests that behaviour needs to be reinterpreted and seen as deliberate, purposeful behaviour. This chapter explores how we might do this.

From the moment Elsa (16 months) learned to walk, she would toddle into the downstairs cloakroom and pull the toilet paper off its holder. She enjoyed watching it unravel on the floor; and if the toilet roll stopped spinning, she would give it another tug. If her mum rushed in and asked Elsa to stop, Elsa would giggle and laugh and appeared very proud of her achievements!

Charlie (18 months) is sitting in his high chair and deliberately throws his toddler cup from his high chair tray onto the floor, and smiles and laughs as he does so.

His mum picks up the cup and places it back on his tray. Charlie immediately drops the cup again onto the floor. This continues about five more times until Charlie's mum removes the cup from his tray.

Jack (19 months) was building with the bricks and construction materials with two other boys. As soon as they built a tower, Jack deliberately knocked it down. This happened repeatedly and the two boys got cross with Jack. He responded saying, 'Down, down.' Later on, Jack found some models that other children had made out of junk materials and he proceeded to take them apart. The other children found this upsetting and Jack's key person felt concerned about the destructive nature of his play.

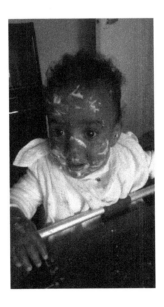

Cassie (9 months) was learning to feed herself with a spoon, however she preferred using her hands to smear yoghurt all over her face. She repeated this every time that she was given yoghurt!

At nursery, Katie (3 years 10 months) loves to pull all of the tissues out of the tissue box repeatedly. The room supervisor asks her to stop and has now placed the tissue boxes out of reach.

During free-play time, Isaac (4 years 8 months) and Zac (5 years 1 month) were plugging the classroom sink with green paper towels. They scrunched up paper towels and pushed then down into the plughole, then turned the tap on. Mrs Brown asked them what they were doing and Isaac said, 'We're making a dam for all the water.'

Here are a few scenarios that could be deemed as challenging or disobedient but are actually schematic. You may see children:

- pulling all the tissues out of the tissue box (trajectory, containing)

- unravelling the toilet roll (core and radial, rotation)

- emptying boxes or tipping all of the toys onto the floor (containing)

- knocking down towers (trajectory, connecting)

- dismantling things and taking things apart (connecting)

- throwing cup or toy from high chair (trajectory)

- plugging sinks with paper (containing, going through a boundary)

- playing with running water (trajectory)

- mixing sand and water together (transforming)

- pouring their drink onto their food (transforming)

- smearing food over their faces, hands and bodies (enveloping)

- filling pockets or bags with sticks and stones (containing)
- collecting toys and resources in bags or other containers and moving them around the setting (containing)
- playing with doors or gates (going through a boundary)
- not wanting food to touch other foods on the plate (positioning)
- only wanting a certain coloured plate or cup (positioning)
- playing with the curtains (enveloping)
- tipping the contents of your handbag onto the floor (containing).

So what? Re-interpreting behaviour as schematic

When parents and practitioners first hear about schemas, they often have a 'lightbulb' moment as they suddenly realise that some behaviours that they were finding particularly difficult to cope with are, in fact, schematic. Understanding schemas can provide us with insights into why children do the things they do and, if necessary, help us to redirect their behaviour into more meaningful or appropriate activities.

These behaviours can be challenging, frustrating and annoying and can make the adult's life difficult when caring for young children. However, the key is in this phrase, 'make the adult's life difficult'. Children will behave in these ways. First, we need to accept this; then, we need to find a way of embracing these behaviours. Sometimes we may need to redirect children to other activities in order to keep them safe; however, if the child's behaviour is only inconveniencing us, we should simply plan for it. That way, we will be ready to work with these schemas and support and extend the child's behaviour rather than try to stop it.

Take Charlie, for example, who we first met in Chapter 1. The more the parent tries to stop the act of throwing, the more he enjoys the game that is being shared. Offering him alternative games that do not involve trajectory movements will probably not satisfy his urge to throw and it could result in an upset child and frustrated parent. With an understanding of schemas, we can observe his play and interpret it as learning about the world and how things work, investigating cause and effect, forces like gravity, and ideas such as object permanence. Charlie's mum plays along for a short while – perhaps with a greater understanding of why Charlie is behaving in this way, she may have been willing to play for longer. The same would apply to Joshua in Chapter 12, who was throwing his toys out of his cot. If his parent understood that this is a valuable game to play, he and his sister would have been able to play for longer. This was also a very social experience for Joshua and his sister as they were engaging in shared communication through the game.

Elsa enjoys watching the toilet paper unravel and pile up on the floor. She may be interested in how the toilet roll spins on the holder, thus indicating an interest in rotation, or she may be interested in the trajectory movement of pulling the toilet paper, which could also indicate an interest in core and radial or trajectory schemas. She is not only learning about cause and effect and the force that is needed to pull the paper, but also how her mum responds to her efforts. She clearly likes the attention and finds the whole situation highly amusing!

Jack's key person was concerned by the destructive nature of Jack's play, continually knocking towers down; however, in my experience, this is a phase that children can go through while investigating disconnecting. We have already identified that Jack has a keen connection schema as we have observed him connecting and disconnecting the fences pieces (see Chapter 3); thus it should come as no surprise that Jack also wants to disconnect towers by knocking them down. Jack also enjoys trajectory movement (see Chapter 12) and the process of knocking down a tower combines disconnecting with movement, connecting and trajectory schemas. Jack is investigating these schemas in different contexts and working out what happens when he pushes the tower. Will the pieces fall down and land at the same time? Do I need to push the tower hard or gently? Will it make a sound? He is beginning to think about force, gravity and connectivity.

Katie's behaviour in pulling all the tissues out of the box is very frustrating for the practitioners. It is wasteful of both money and resources and might mean that there are not any tissues available when one is needed for blowing a child's nose. However, we have already identified that she has a strong containing schema and loves to engage with filling and emptying containers (see Chapter 4). In her eyes, why shouldn't she empty this tissue box? She is investigating the action of pulling and emptying. What happens when the tissues run out? Often a new box of tissues 'magically' appears and Katie can begin the process again!

Cassie enjoys smearing yoghurt all over her face and this could be interpreted as misbehaviour. I have heard some parents and practitioners chastise very young children for covering their faces, hands and bodies with food. However, just like Cassie, these children are not being deliberately disobedient; rather, they are exploring textures and the feeling of covering themselves with a substance. It is related to the enveloping schema and in Chapter 7 we observed that Cassie enjoys exploring the feeling of being covered up as she plays in her ball pool.

Isaac and Zac are undertaking a scientific investigation about how the water remains in the sink when they plug it with paper. They are beginning to investigate water pressure and water flow. Playing with water is often trajectory as children are interested in the movement or flow of water; however, this could also be containing play, as indicated by Isaac's language as he talks about dams. We met Isaac in Chapter 4 and identified that he has a keen interest in containing, so this fits with our previous knowledge of him.

What next? Extending schematic behaviour

We can intervene in children's exploratory play in attuned ways through applying our knowledge and understanding of schematic behaviour to extend and develop children's play further. However, sometimes we need to stand back and not intervene too quickly (see Chapter 2). This is a skill that is difficult to master – knowing when or whether to intervene. Julie Fisher[4] uses the phrase 'interacting or interfering' which sums this up perfectly!

Charlie's mum might want to encourage him to engage in other activities that involve cause and effect, such as playing with some mechanical or technological toys which move or respond when you touch a button. Alternatively, she might want to tap into his interest in trajectory movement and offer him opportunities to play throwing games with toys, for example, by giving him a toy that she doesn't mind being thrown from the high chair (she could swap it with the cup every time he wants to play the game).

We can tap into Elsa's potential interest in rolling and unrolling things by offering her rolling pins to use with playdough. We could also allow her to play with a toilet roll outside the toilet area. This could become Elsa's special toilet roll that she can unroll at her leisure. Perhaps her mum could encourage her to roll it up again so she has the opportunity to unroll it again. Every time that Elsa unrolls the toilet paper roll in the bathroom or toilet area, she can be directed to her special toilet roll, which she has permission to unroll. Over time Elsa will learn that she can unroll the special one but not the others.

Jack will relish additional opportunities to build and construct using a variety of materials. We can work alongside Jack to help him to understand how the action of knocking down a tower impacts on the other children. Many young children find it difficult to empathise and will need support from an adult to develop empathy.

We can build on Katie's interest in containing by offering her different-sized containers to fill to her heart's content. In order to encourage her not to pull out the tissues from the tissue box, we can present Katie with her own tissue box to decorate. We can explain that she must not pull the tissues out of the plain boxes because the other children and grown-ups need to use these tissues, but instead Katie is allowed to pull the tissues out of her own special box. We can then encourage Katie to put the tissues back into the box and tell her that her special tissue box is available to be used next time she feels the urge to pull all the tissues out of a different box.

If we consider Cassie's interest in smearing yoghurt all over her face, I understand that some adults may want to discourage this behaviour; however, we can still encourage her to participate in this type of play. We could offer her opportunities to play with soap bubbles in the bath, covering her face and body with bubbles, or we might want to introduce her to other types of messy play and accept that it is likely that she'll cover her face or body with mess. So we can plan for this, have plenty of wipes and a change of clothes to hand, or provide waterproof suits or long-sleeved aprons for her to wear during messy play. If Cassie was still very hungry she would be eating the yoghurt, so we can also assume that she has finished her meal, offer her another spoonful to make sure and then check, 'Have you finished eating? Oh, you want to play with the yoghurt now? OK.' With a child as young as Cassie you may also want to consider using sign language to reinforce your words.

If we were concerned that Isaac and Zac could clog or block the sink by continuing with their investigation, we might want to suggest that they continue this investigation using the water tray and use the plughole in the bottom of it. They could extend their play by trying different materials and investigating whether or not they act as good plugs. Would a sponge work well? What about a large stone? What material do they think would stop the flow of water best? Why?

Clearly there are times when a child is engaging in an unsafe action or their behaviour may disrupt or hurt others and this needs to be stopped, regardless of whether or not it is schematic. Most practitioners have developed a range of strategies to use in such situations, like a simple *ABC analysis* which considers the Antecedents, Behaviour and Consequences, looking into the incident in detail using detective skills to unpick possible causes and triggers for the behaviour (see Chapter 2). Mollie in Chapter 8 had a keen interest in doors and doorways and we can use this schematic play to help her learn strategies to keep herself safe, while offering her doorways that she can travel through to satisfy her urge to go through doors. Tapping into children's schematic interests can help to redirect or channel the children's energies into a more appropriate and safer activity. Cathy Nutbrown[5] suggests that 'many professional educators use what they know of schemas to divert children from disruptive activities and to focus them on more worthwhile endeavours.'

Understanding schemas will not answer all challenging behaviours displayed by children. However, parents and practitioners need to be discerning and scratch beneath the surface of such behaviour to see if there is, indeed, purpose in their activity. In doing so, they may identify schemas and can reinterpret children's behaviour in a positive light; they can then use this knowledge to build upon the children's fascinations and redirect the behaviour into more meaningful pursuits.

Practitioners and parents can feel reassured, relieved even, when they realise that these behaviours are normal and an accepted, often expected, part of child development. By interpreting these repetitive actions as schemas, the interest that these children have demonstrated through their behaviour becomes understood, forgiven and hopefully catered for in other ways. We can also see children as co-constructors of knowledge and competent learners.

Respecting children

When we try to understand schemas from a child's perspective, we respect the child's views. This mirrors the Mosaic approach,[6] which sees young children as 'experts in their own lives', 'skillful communicators', 'active participants' and 'meaning makers, researchers, and explorers'. It places the views of young children at the centre and attempts to listen and respond to children's perspectives.

If we relate this to Jack, who had the urge to knock down towers and take other children's creations apart, we can view him as a competent learner. He is using a range of communication strategies through his behaviour and words to make his ideas about disconnection understood. He actively participated by investigating and exploring the concept of 'falling down', thus searching for meaning through his research. By acknowledging what the children are trying to achieve, we respect their thoughts and actions.

In the case of Isaac and Zac, their learning and investigation could have been halted if their teacher did not permit playing in the sink, misinterpreting the play as unconstructive. However, the exploration was very meaningful and purposeful to these children and could lead on to other investigations and a huge amount of learning.

Thinking about children and their behaviour in this way is not a new phenomenon! Maria Montessori[7] stated back in 1936 that it is easy to attribute puzzling reactions and difficult phases to naughtiness. Instead of this stance, she chose to view children's behaviour as 'a problem that must be solved, an enigma that must be deciphered'. This is more challenging for the adult as we become more of a student of the child than a judge. We must be open to learn and observe and have a yearning to decipher and understand children's perplexing and challenging behaviour. If we genuinely want to provide learning experiences that are meaningful to the children in our care, we need to have an understanding of schemas in order to respond appropriately.

References

1. Page, J., Clare, A. and Nutbrown, C. (2013) *Working with Babies and Children from Birth to Three* (2nd ed.). London: Sage.
2. NDNA (2016) *Schemas: what we can learn from children's behaviour patterns* (schemas app). Retrieved from www.ndna.org.uk/NDNA/Training/Schemas_app.aspx, on 27 February 2017.
3. Athey, C. (2007) *Extending Thought in Young Children: A Parent–Teacher Partnership* (2nd ed.). London: Sage.
4. Fisher, J. (2016) *Interacting or Interfering? Improving Interactions in the Early Years*. Maidenhead: Open University Press.
5. Nutbrown, C. (2011) *Threads of Thinking* (4th ed.), p.22. London: Sage.
6. Clark, A. and Moss, P. (2011) *Listening to Young Children: The Mosaic Approach* (2nd ed.). London: NCB.
7. Montessori, M. (1936) *The Secret of Childhood*, p.66. London: Longmans, Green and Co.

Chapter 16

In Summary

CHAPTER OBJECTIVE

This final chapter will summarise the key points from within the book, reiterating that children can be involved with more than one schema at a time and that some schematic behaviour can be misinterpreted as naughtiness. It will also offer a few questions for reflection.

Schemas are simply patterns of repeated behaviour and thinking which help the child to understand the world through exploration and investigation. Some children clearly follow one schema, for example, Noah, John and Caitlin; others more than one schema at once, for example, Katie, Jack, Juliette and Carlos, while other children we observe may not follow any at all. Overall, within the early years age group it is common for children to exhibit schematic behaviour and this should not be considered as concerning or worrying by parents or practitioners. Schemas are an interesting part of many children's development.

Over the past few years schemas have been increasing in popularity and influence. Early years practitioners can attend training courses and conferences which address these issues and there are even apps[1] that practitioners and parents can download which help them to identify schematic behaviour in their children. Such tools and training opportunities support adults in their role of identifying schemas and supporting children as they pursue their fascinations.

When parents and practitioners have an understanding of schemas, it helps them to:

- understand why children do certain things and behave in certain ways

- have a clear focus for observing children

- get to know their children better in terms of their interests and fascinations

- use a new language that better describes children's actions and behaviours

- plan appropriate opportunities to support and extend children's learning

- provide more open-ended opportunities for learning

- provide an enabling environment within which children can explore and investigate

- see the value in repetitive play which will strengthen the neural pathways in children's brains

- share their understanding about schemas with other parents and professionals

- see children as competent learners and co-constructors of knowledge.

I believe that there is a need to evangelise regarding schemas in order to offer a new interpretation of children's behaviour. Schema theory needs to be made more accessible to practitioners and parents alike and it is my hope that this book has begun this process. The real strength of considering schemas and schematic behaviour actually lies within practice rather than in theory. Nutbrown[2] supports this idea, stating, 'Knowledge of schemas can better enable educators to teach in ways that are attuned to the structures of individual children's thinking and action.' It is how the adults use their knowledge to fine-tune their interactions with children in practice that is the key.

Tuning into children's interests and fascinations is part of daily practice for those working with or caring for young children. Now that you have read this book, you will also be identifying schemas and tuning into them. When adults observe children closely, with the intent of finding out and understanding their forms of thought, it is as if they are scientists. As Gopnik, Meltzoff and Kuhl[3] state so eloquently:

> The scientist peering into the crib, looking for answers to some of the deepest questions about how minds, and the world and language work, sees the scientist peering out of the crib, who, it turns out, is doing much the same thing. No wonder they both smile.

Practitioners and parents investigate children, who in turn are using schemas to investigate the world. They are both actively participating in this process.

Questions for reflection

- Have you identified any schematic behaviour?

- What do you think the child is investigating?

- Can you describe the learning that is taking place?

- How can you support and extend the child's fascinations?

- How is the learning environment enabling and supporting these schemas?

- What activities and resources cater for children's interests, schemas, fascinations and individual needs?

- Are you confident in your knowledge and understanding of child development to assess schematic behaviour?

- Are there any challenging behaviours displayed that are probably schematic?

- How can you further support children and redirect this behaviour?

When a parent or practitioner first finds out about schemas, they often have a eureka moment as they begin to understand some of the behaviours and actions of children that had previously appeared bizarre or even concerning. The next step is to become an evangelist, telling the world about this new understanding! The more people that find out about schemas, the more widely this information will be spread and the more children will be better understood. It is my hope that this book will help to do just that. So spread the word about schemas!

References

1. NDNA (2016) *Schemas: what we can learn from children's behaviour patterns* (schemas app). Retrieved from www.ndna.org.uk/NDNA/Training/Schemas_app.aspx, on 27 February 2017.
2. Nutbrown, C. (2011) *Threads of Thinking* (4th ed.), p.24. London: Sage.
3. Gopnik, A., Meltzoff, A. and Kuhl, P. (2001) *How Babies Think: The Science of Childhood*, pp.3–4. London: Orion Books.

Glossary

ABC or STAR analysis ABC stands for Antecedent, Behaviour, Consequences and STAR stands for Setting, Trigger, Action, Response. These are usually event sampling observation methods which record what happens before, during and after the particular 'event' which is being focused on, for example, a specific behavioural incident. Their main purpose is to find out a reason behind particular behaviours through keeping a detailed record of each event and looking for patterns.

Accommodation When children need to adapt or alter their schemas to accommodate new information.

Amygdala The part of the brain that deals with stress and emotion. Think freeze, fight or flight response.

Assimilation When children come across new information and incorporate it into their schemas.

Autistic Spectrum Disorder (ASD) Also called Autism, this is the collective term for a lifelong developmental condition which covers a wide range of 'symptoms'; hence the term 'spectrum'. Some people with ASD are extremely high functioning, some have specific learning difficulties and some may have mental health issues and anxiety. All people with ASD share difficulties with communication, social interaction and behaviour, although having autism will affect them in different ways. This disability can also be 'hidden' as people with autism do not necessarily look disabled in any way.

Axon A long tentacle-like fibre which extends from the main cell body in a neuron.

Brain plasticity or neuroplasticity This refers to the ability of the brain to organise itself depending on the environment and experiences that it encounters. It refers to the flexibility of the brain and its ability to continue to form synapses throughout a life span.

Dendrites Feather-like receivers which surround the cell body and pick up signals from other neurons.

Forest school This is a type of outdoor learning (for all ages – nursery to adult) replicating teaching in Denmark which uses the outdoor environment, specifically forests and woodland, to teach children practical skills and build their self-esteem and independence. Typically, children who participate in forest school activities go out in all weathers and engage in risky play within the safe boundaries that are set by the practitioners.

Formative assessment This is the process of seeking and interpreting evidence for use by children and their practitioners to determine where the learners are in their learning, where they need to go next and how best to get there, for example, observing children during play, thinking about what you have seen and using this knowledge to plan the next steps in their learning and development.

Heuristic play This term was first used by Elinor Goldschmeid, a child psychologist, and describes what happens when young children are offered 'real' objects to play with in an open-ended way, for example, gathering a collection of balls of different sizes and textures and presenting them to children in a basket, so that the children can explore and investigate and lead the play in whichever direction they want to.

Kinaesthesia This is your awareness of your body movement. It goes hand in hand with proprioception (see proprioceptive sense below) and the terms have even been used interchangeably.

Limbic system This is a collective term used to describe some mental functions of the brain responsible for emotions, learning and memory. It includes the amygdala, basal ganglia, cingulate gyrus, hippocampus, hypothalamus and thalamus, which are all parts of the brain located beneath the cerebrum (the largest part of the brain, divided into left and right hemispheres).

Myelination This term describes the process of a fatty substance that builds up around the axon of a neuron, acting like an insulator and enabling signals to pass along the axon more efficiently.

Neural plate The part of the brain that develops first in an embryo. The majority of neurons or brain cells come from the neural plate.

Neuron Also called neurone or nerve cell, this is a cell that can transmit information through electrical and chemical signals via synapses.

Planning cycle/OAP cycle This is when practitioners Observe children, Assess what they can do and use this knowledge to Plan future learning opportunities for their children. It is a cycle because when we implement this planning we observe children again.

Proprioceptive sense This is your ability to know where your body is situated in space. If you close your eyes and put your hand up, do you still know where your hand is? Most people will still know that their hand is up without having to look. This is proprioception.

Scaffolding In order to support children we offer them additional materials, ask questions or make suggestions to help them to progress in their learning. This is a bit like actual scaffolding, when a building needs support around it.

Summative assessment Summative assessment is any assessment that summarises where learners are at a given point in time – it provides a snapshot of what has been learned in terms of attainment and achievement. Tick-lists of achievement, tests and exams are all forms of summative assessment.

Sustained shared thinking This describes the process when two or more people discuss an issue, problem or concept to extend and further develop children's thinking. This phrase arose out of the Effective Provision of Preschool Education (EPPE) research, which began in 2003.

Synapses This term is used to describe the process of passing electrical or chemical signals from one neuron to another. Although they make a connection, the word connection is misleading as there is a tiny synaptic gap between the neurons over which the signals pass.

Synaptic gap A tiny gap between neurons, which information can be shared across through electrical impulses.

Synaptic pruning From an early age until late adolescence, the brain 'prunes' away any synapses that are not sufficiently strong or have been used very infrequently. Strong synapses are exempt from this process. The resulting brain has fewer synapses but this fine-tuning has made it more efficient.

Vestibular system This is situated in the inner ear and is primarily responsible for balance, coordination and spatial orientation.

Zone of Proximal Development Vygotsky came up with a model based on three concentric circles – in the centre we have what a child can do by themselves, the middle ring is what a child can do with support and the outside ring is what a child cannot yet do. This middle ring is the zone of proximal development. Working in this zone, we are trying to offer children opportunities through what we provide for them in the environment or plan for them to do in activities that will extend their thinking and enable them to achieve more than they would have achieved alone.

Index

Coral, 134
  rotation schema, 129, 132
core and radial schema, 68, 169, 171
  case studies, 69–71
  example activities, 71–2
  extending, 73–5
  interpreting, 72–3
  links with other schemas, 76
  observing, 68–72
  rotation schema and, 138
  suggested activities, 74–5
  trajectory schema and, 149
counting, 123
covering up, 87
creating, 27
creations
  as documentation, 42
critical thinking, 27–8, 32
Cubey, P., 12

dendrites, 23
Deon
  trajectory schema, 140, 145
Department for Education (DfE) (2014), 16
Department for Education (DfE) (2017), 16
Development Matters non-statutory guidance, 16
Dexter, 114, 138
  orientation schema, 113
disconnecting schema, 52, 57, 59, 171
distance, 162
distraction
  from schematic behaviours, 19
documentation
  benefits for children, 40–1
  methods of, 42
  purposes, 37
doors and windows
  fascination with, 98, 102
  safety issues, 103

early brain development, 21–7
Early Education (2012), 16
Early Years Foundation Stage (EYFS), 16
effective learning, 27–8
  characteristics, 32, 39
Effective Provision in Pre-school Education (EPPE), 14
Elsa, 173
  case study, 167
  reinterpreting schematic behaviour, 171
Emily, 36
empathy
  developing, 174
enclosing schema, 102
  case studies, 78–80
  containing schema and, 66, 67
  enveloping schema and, 96
  example activities, 80–1
  extending, 83–4
  going through a boundary schema and, 106
  interpreting, 81–2
  links with other schemas, 86
  observing, 77–81
  positioning schema and, 123
  suggested activities, 84–5
engagement, 28
enveloping schema, 87, 169, 170
  case studies, 88–91
  enclosing schema and, 77, 86
  example activities, 91
  extending, 93–5
  interpreting, 92–3
  links with other schema, 96
  observing, 87–91
  suggested activities, 94–5
  trajectory schema and, 149
Ethan, 135, 138
  rotation schema, 130–1, 133
eureka moment, 13, 181

Ewan
  positioning schema, 119, 123
example activities
  connecting schema, 51–2
  containing schema, 61–2
  core and radial schema, 71–2
  enclosing schema, 80–1
  enveloping schema, 91
  going through a boundary schema, 101
  orientation schema, 112
  rotation schema, 151–2
  trajectory schema, 142
  transforming schema, 153–4
  transporting schema, 161
extending, 181
  children's learning, 36
  connecting schema, 54–6
  containing schema, 64–6
  core and radial schema, 73–5
  enclosing schema, 83–5
  enveloping schema, 93–5
  going through a boundary schema, 103–6
  orientation schema, 114–16
  positioning schema, 124–6
  rotation schema, 134–7
  thinking, 15
  trajectory schema, 145–8
  transforming schema, 155–7
  transporting schema, 162–4

fascination
  attuning to children's, 29
  good learning and, 28
fine motor skills, 82
Fisher, J., 173
foot-eye coordination, 143

Observation, Assessment
and Planning (OAP
cycle), 32
observational assessment,
43
one-to-one
correspondence, 123
open-ended questions, 14
ordering and classifying,
121
containing schema
and, 64
ordering and sequencing,
122
organisational skills, 122
orientation schema, 107,
108, 138
case studies, 109–11
example activities, 112
extending, 114–16
interpreting, 112–14
links with other
schemas, 117
observing, 108–12
positioning schema
and, 127
suggested activities,
114–16
outside agencies
sharing with, 45

Page, J., 166
parent comments, 42
parent-carer interactions,
43, 45
peek-a-boo play, 92, 106
Penn Green Team, 16
photographs
annotated, 41, 42
use in observation, 37
Piaget, J., 12, 113
planning, 32
future learning
opportunities, 40
next steps, 44
in OAP cycle, 33
observation and, 33
planning cycle, 32, 33
play
repetitive, 11
playing and exploring
effective learning
through, 27
positioning schema, 55,
107, 118, 179
case studies, 119–21
connecting schema
and, 57

containing schema and,
66, 67
enclosing schema and,
86
enveloping schema
and, 92
example activities,
121–2
extending, 124–6
interpreting, 122–4
links with other
schemas, 127
observing, 118–22
orientation schema
and, 117
suggested activities,
125–6
problem solving, 39
proprioceptive sense, 123,
132, 144

questioning, 34
observation and, 33
questions
abstract, 15
concrete, 15
open-ended, 14
questions for reflection,
181

Rachel
mud play, 31
reciprocity
and learning capacity,
28
recording
observation and, 33
redirection, 175, 181
reflectiveness, 46
and learning capacity,
28
repeated experiences
learning through, 24
processing speed and,
24
synaptic development
and, 28
repetition
connection-making
and, 25
repetitive behaviour, 12,
17, 144, 176
repetitive play, 11
resilience
and learning capacity,
28
resourcefulness

and learning capacity,
28
risk management, 144
rituals, 123
Rose, S., 15
Rosen, M., 94
rotation schema, 11, 15,
34, 45, 128, 169
case studies, 129–31
combining with
trajectory schema,
68
core and radial schema
and, 76
example activities,
151–2
extending, 134–7
interpreting, 132–3
links with other
schemas, 138
observing, 128–32
suggested activities,
135–7
transporting schema
and, 165
routines, 123
changing, 45

Sally, 117
orientation schema, 109
Sammy
orientation schema,
110–11, 114, 115
trajectory schema, 141,
145
Sarah, 24
scaffolding, 14, 15
schema theory, 180
schemas, 11
absence from early
childhood
programmes, 17
benefits of
understanding, 179
connecting, 49–57
core and radial, 68–76
defined, 12–15, 16
in early years
frameworks, 16–17
enclosing, 77–86
enveloping schema,
87–97
as forms of thought, 12
going through a
boundary, 98–107
identifying, 17, 35, 44
observing, 30
orientation, 108–17